Date Due

Success in Teaching
SCHOOL ORCHESTRAS
AND BANDS

Success in Teaching
SCHOOL ORCHESTRAS
AND BANDS

by

CHARLES BOARDMAN RIGHTER

ASSOCIATE PROFESSOR OF MUSIC
AND DIRECTOR OF BANDS
STATE UNIVERSITY OF IOWA

Paul A. Schmitt Music Company
MINNEAPOLIS

DEDICATED
TO THE
AMATEUR MUSICIANS
OF
AMERICA

Preface

This work is intended primarily for those conductors of high school, college and community orchestras and bands who believe that the performance of amateur musicians can be carried beyond the limits ordinarily attained by such organizations. The results which have been achieved in recent years by the best of these groups have approached the highest standard of professional excellence. Some of those which have failed to reach an acceptable level of accomplishment have been handicapped by poor facilities and equipment while others have lacked competent leadership.

Method, as such, is a weak and ineffective tool in the hands of one who does not possess the skill of a fine craftsman or the soul of an artist. Not all can be endowed with these qualities, but there are few who lack the capacity to improve their craftsmanship and enrich their artistry through practice and study.

On the well-worn theory that a thing which is worth doing at all is worth doing well, the conductor owes it to himself and to his profession to discover, if possible, the causes of failure or half-success. If these causes are external—if they arise outside the rehearsal—the remedies must be sought elsewhere; but if the fault exists in the person of the conductor himself, only rigid self-analysis and the gradual improvement of his teaching technique will remedy the situation.

Many books have been written on the general subject of conducting, and a number dealing with problems of organization and management are also available. While such works are invaluable aids to the orchestra or band conductor, guidance in the actual process of developing playing skills and interpretation is of equal importance. It is one thing for the conductor to have a complete mastery of musical fundamentals but quite a different thing for him to possess the ability to transmit this knowledge to those under his direction. To help the conductor in the accomplishment of this task is the underlying purpose of this text.

The work makes no pretense to completeness—the subject is far too broad for the attainment of such a goal. If the material is not as meticulously organized as might be desired, this is because so much of it defies rigid classification. The predominant hope is that somewhere within the volume the reader will find a few practical ideas, suggestions, or techniques which may be applicable in his own teaching.

The assistance of the following individuals is hereby acknowledged and recorded: Miriam Williams Righter, V. Evelyn Powers, Arnold L. Oehlson, and Frederick W. Kent. Permission to use certain copyrighted materials has been granted by the following firms:

Associated Music Publishers, Inc., New York.
C. L. Barnhouse Co., Oskaloosa, Iowa.
Oliver Ditson Co., Philadelphia.
Carl Fischer, Inc., New York.
Music Publishers Holding Corporation, New York.

THE AUTHOR

Iowa City, Iowa

Contents

CHAPTER I

Training of the Instrumental Teacher

Music was first formally introduced into the public schools of America in Boston in the year 1838 but until near the close of the century its place in the curriculum was relatively unimportant and any achievements worthy of note could be traced to the energy and enthusiasm of widely dispersed individual teachers. However, methods of teaching vocal music were improved during this period and the stage was set for general expansion of the music program. A few small orchestras were organized about 1900, and some years later choruses and glee clubs were given a more secure place in the high school curriculum. At about the same time the more progressive schools began to offer courses in music theory, history, and appreciation. This somewhat general growth of interest in music early in the new century may be traced to a more or less spontaneous recognition of the value of music by the public and by school administrators and to a growing professional consciousness on the part of the music teachers themselves.

The expansion of the school music program continued at an accelerated rate up to the period of World War I and beyond. The two decades following the war witnessed a phenomenal growth in all phases of music education, but particularly in the field of instrumental music. This shift in emphasis from vocal to instrumental has been attributed to the influence of the war and the availability of large numbers of men teachers who had gained specialized instrumental experience in army bands. These may have been contributing factors, but it is more likely that the growth of interest in instrumental music was but a normal phase in the general public acceptance of the importance of music as a basic element in education. The added utility of orchestras and bands in connection with school and community entertainments and other functions, and the broader appeal which this type of participation had for students undoubtedly contributed to the expansion in the instrumental field.

The rapidity with which this new movement for instrumental music training spread through the nation's schools brought with it many problems, some of which have not yet been adequately solved. To the more obvious difficulties of providing suitable space and equipment for large school orchestras and bands was added the lack of properly trained leadership. Of these two needs, the more important was for qualified and experienced leadership — men and women having high artistic ideals, skill as teachers, and the vision and administrative ability necessary to organize the new program. Surely the directorship of, or membership in, an army band could not be said to constitute adequate preparation for this task although such experience might, on occasions, have been found helpful. Among the directors of these post-war school orchestras and bands were also to be found men who had formerly played in theater orchestras or professional and semi-professional concert bands, and many whose principal playing experience had been in dance bands. Still others had been private teachers of instrumental music before the war. Only in the rarest cases were there to be found teachers whose previous experience would fully qualify them to undertake the many-sided task of organizing a new program, teaching the various instruments in beginning classes, selecting music suitable for amateur performance, and working smoothly with school faculties and parents in a project that was little understood by any of those concerned.

It is to the credit of these early teachers of instrumental music that they succeeded in surmounting the many obstacles which they encountered in those first years following the establishment of the new program. Theirs was a problem of adaptation seldom encountered in the educational field; and, in tribute, it may be said that they bridged the gap with marked resourcefulness and ingenuity.

In fact, so well did these novice teachers do their work that most school administrators and teacher-training institutions never did discover the fundamental inadequacies in their training or that of their immediate successors in the field. The next generation of instrumental teachers entered the field with only slightly more real training than was enjoyed by these pioneers, although they did have the advantage of a growing tradition in the field and an established pattern of organization. True, more music was being taught in colleges and universities, and requirements for graduation in music courses were expanded; but still there was little real training provided in the specific techniques of teaching beginners in mixed classes, conducting, organizing instrumental courses of study, selecting suitable music, arranging, and the like. The instrumental teacher and director was still, in large measure, a man without a country so far as his educational preparation was concerned. Requirements for certification and for graduation from conservatories, colleges, and universities lagged far behind the actual needs, and the emphasis remained upon one's fitness to teach or supervise vocal music. Even for students majoring in instrumental music the ability to play a single instrument was generally accepted as meeting the requirements, and few, if any, practical courses were offered in the field of instrumental teaching or conducting. In those few institutions which first began to sense the real nature of the problem, the instrumental course (if such it could be called) was usually superimposed upon the established course for vocal teachers and was more often than not too restricted to be of much value. This weakness in the preparation of teachers of instrumental music still prevails after more than a quarter century in which teacher-training institutions have had an opportunity to study the needs of the instrumental field. Even a casual check will disclose the fact that very few of those who teach instrumental music methods in our colleges and universities have had actual and successful teaching and directing experience in elementary and secondary schools.

As a consequence of this generally faulty guidance on the part of teacher-training institutions, the instrumental teacher and supervisor has usually been forced to enter the field with a totally inadequate advance preparation; and he has usually found it necessary to continue his own training while trying to teach others. This burdensome and unsatisfactory road to professional advancement should be avoided at all costs, since even with the best of preliminary training the young teacher faces a trying period of orientation in his first teaching assignment. One whose advance training has been partially or wholly lacking in its essential elements could not fail to experience the greatest difficulty in adjusting himself to a situation which demands, even of the best, a high degree of teaching skill and organizing ability. Failure to make such adjustments inevitably involves the teacher in a false attitude toward his work and toward his students and colleagues. The immediate effect is discouragement and disillusionment which all too often either rob the profession of a potentially valuable member or reduce the teacher's effectiveness more or less permanently, depending upon his temperamental resilience. Many a promising young teacher has had his chances for a successful career materially lessened as a result of faulty or inadequate professional training at the time of his assuming a position of major responsibility. That many have achieved the outward appearance of success in spite of this lack neither justifies nor excuses the practice as even these have learned their job at the expense of their students.

It is questionable whether any teacher has the capacity to satisfy all of the demands of a full-time teaching position and at the same time master the techniques of new instruments, acquire a comprehensive knowledge of current teaching materials, familiarize himself with progressive methods of teaching, perfect his conducting technique, and advance his own musicianship. At some of these points there are bound to be lapses and omissions which will definitely limit the effectiveness of the individual as a teacher and conductor. Even under the most favorable circumstances there will remain a vast body of knowledge, skill, and experience to be gained after one has launched his professional career.

Growth in musicianship and expansion of aptitudes and techniques are continuing processes which are closely allied with the daily routine of teaching. In fact, the presence or absence of this factor of personal and professional improvement in service may well mark the difference between success and failure in a teaching career, regardless of the extent of one's advance preparation. It is even conceivable that one with a relatively inadequate background might sharply outdistance a more favored competitor through continued private study and the application of the principle of day-by-day self-improvement. Ideally, the training of the teacher should consist of two coordinated parts — an adequate undergraduate course and a planned program of post graduate study along professional lines. The former should include, in addition to the usual cultural and technical studies, extensive opportunities for laboratory teaching under experienced and competent supervision, to be followed upon entrance into active teaching by further study with private teachers, active participation in clinical meetings and teachers' conferences, enrollment for special summer courses, and rigid adherence to a program of professional reading and the study of recorded music. The practical considerations involved in the formulation and application of such an intensive plan must inevitably prove difficult; but the chief obstacle rests in the failure of teacher-training institutions, teacher-hiring agencies, and the individual teacher to appreciate fully the need of a broader concept of musical leadership and greater technical skill in teaching.

The more ambitious and progressive teachers of instrumental music have generally recognized the nature of their own problem and have taken whatever means were possible to remedy shortcomings in their professional training. Many have enrolled for graduate courses in universities where they have more often than not been obliged to take the chaff of outmoded and stereotyped "required courses" along with the wheat of practical seminar and laboratory groups designed to meet and solve specific problems of everyday teaching. Others have sought the private studio teacher with results as variable as are the abilities and philosophies of these individuals. Some, in more isolated areas, have been forced to depend upon their own resources with the aid of recordings, textbooks, and intensive practice. The widely prevalent desire for self-improvement and professional growth is attested by the increase (before World War II) in the number of so-called instrumental clinics under the sponsorship of teachers' organizations and educational institutions. All of these devices, methods, and agencies have accounted for a tremendous advance in the competence of individual teachers and explain, in large measure, the ability of the high school students, under the tutelage of these progressive teachers, to master most of the technical difficulties of the standard orchestral and band literature. The students' appreciation of the musical values inherent in these same works is another question entirely. As one discerning authority stated after hearing a group of soloists in a national contest: "They exhibit to an amazing degree *practiced accuracy in execution*, but little *sense of musicianship*." The teachers of these students deserve a full measure of credit for their accuracy in execution, but they must also accept the responsibility for their lack of musicianship. It is in this realm of interpretation, or sensitivity to musical values as such, that our training processes have failed most noticeably if we are to judge by the considered opinions of the many excellent musicians who have been privileged to hear all classes of instrumental groups under the most favorable circumstances.

Problems of technical and musical pedagogy will be treated in greater detail in later chapters of this work. In fact, almost the sole justification for these writings is to interpret the teaching of both mechanical performance and interpretation, as well as some matters of organization and supervision of instrumental groups, in terms of more or less specific techniques. But before delving too deeply into these problems it is important to consider a question which may be regarded as of equally fundamental importance in determining the success or failure of an individual in a field in which qualities of personality and professional fitness are curiously and inexplicably intertwined. This general question might be defined as having to do with the attitude of the teacher toward his profession and his innate aptitude for the work which he has chosen.

The music teaching profession is not unlike other professions, skilled trades, and business callings in that it has attracted many who possess neither a marked aptitude for, nor a thoroughly satisfactory attitude toward, the specific niche they are required to fill. Gross inefficiency and widespread unhappiness are the natural and inescapable consequences of this all-too-common state in which square pegs are trying to fit themselves into round holes, and vice versa. The problem is not so acute where an *almost* round peg is fitted into the round hole or where a slightly irregular square peg is inserted into the square hole. These cases involve unnecessary friction, wasted energy, and a generally unsatisfactory final result; but outwardly, at least, the faulty alignment and the loss of operating efficiency are apt to be overlooked.

Some years ago a number of alert business concerns began to pioneer in the realm of psychological research as a means of insuring greater efficiency and a larger measure of personal satisfaction on the part of employees through better selection of personnel and more suitable work assignments. With the inauguration of the selective service law shortly before this country's entrance into World War II, the government instituted a similar program of personal aptitude study on a scale almost unbelievably penetrating and exhaustive. The purpose of this intensive analysis of each prospective soldier's individual capabilities — physical, mental, and emotional — was threefold: (1) to save time by finding the man best suited to each particular job and the one who could learn a new job most readily, (2) to avoid the waste of manpower and materiel which inevitably resulted when an inept person was assigned a task beyond his comprehension, and (3) to make each soldier feel that his contribution was of major importance to the war effort. This last consideration was perhaps of the greatest importance because it brought to the individual a measure of personal satisfaction and pride in his work. To say that the methods used in determining fitness or that the interpretations placed upon the psychological findings were universally correct would be a far too optimistic evaluation of the entire project, but the fact remains that the procedure was based upon fundamentally sound principles and undoubtedly served its essential purposes.

In contrast with these examples of the utilization of scientific processes in the selection and assignment of personnel, consider the hit-or-miss methods by which teachers find their way into our educational institutions. Very few colleges and universities make any attempt to go beyond the formal entrance requirements in the acceptance of students; and in most instances students are permitted to select their major courses with only a minimum of guidance and no exhaustive investigation into their technical, intellectual, or temperamental fitness for the particular field. The notable exceptions to this rule will be found in most medical schools and a relatively few colleges of dentistry, engineering, and other specialized branches.

In most institutions granting degrees in music, the principal conditions imposed upon the entering student are an interest in the subject, some performing ability upon an instrument, and the ability to pay for the required private lessons. Once accepted, he need only demonstrate a reasonable rate of progress, pass certain required courses, and possibly present a senior recital. Little distinction is made between students of outstanding native capacity and a fine background of early study, and those who enter college or university with the barest minimum of preliminary musical training. At no point in the college course is there any effective barrier to the student's progress toward eventual graduation. True, the head of the department may have the authority to say to the poorly equipped student: "Thus far and no farther!", but he seldom does so. The time for such decisions is either at entrance or within the first year if an unnecessary and unfair hardship is not to be imposed upon the student.

The absence of any satisfactory administrative machinery for determining the capacity of the individual student *before* he completes his college course has accounted for the prevalence of a considerable amount of professional inaptitude among teachers of music as well as in other fields. The widespread failure of teacher-training institutions to recognize this problem, the lack of any central agency to encourage or impose higher standards in the selection of candidates, and the fact that many music teachers have gone through college with no intention or expectation of entering the teaching profession only to drift into the educational field after graduation — all are factors contributing to a somewhat general laxity in the building of a teaching personnel ideally fitted to the specific tasks which they face.

The demands upon the music teacher, and more specifically upon the teacher of instrumental music, are of such a nature that a career in this field cannot be approached casually or through chance. The successful teacher in this field must decide very early in his training period whether he is able and willing to make the necessary sacrifices. He must master the principles and the technique of not one but many instruments, he must usually fit himself for the leadership of both band and orchestra, and he must acquire a broad acquaintanceship with musical literature. All this takes time in the doing; and some years are required for this diversified knowledge and skill to become a part of his experience, i.e., readily available and immediately usable without reference to texts, fingering charts, prepared teaching guides, or other sources of information. When one considers the time required to master even the minimum fundamentals of any one instrument (sufficient for essential demonstrations in connection with teaching), the need of a prolonged period of preparation for the general instrumental teacher is more fully appreciated. The teacher's first position will usually require that he teach beginners at all grade levels, either as individuals or in mixed groups; consequently, he must know thoroughly the technique of not less than sixteen different types of instruments. In the smaller towns the school music supervisor or instrumental teacher will usually have to depend entirely upon his own resources, as few private teachers will be available and these will generally be performers on the more common instruments only. Too often the young teacher thinks of himself as a conductor, not as a teacher; but he will soon discover that his principal responsibility is in the field of teaching. In fact, he will never find himself in a position in which a knowledge of the instruments and the ability to teach them are not considerations of paramount importance. The finest university band or orchestra would deteriorate at a rapid rate were the conductor not able to teach as he conducts, and this means that he must deal with actual and sometimes very elementary technical problems in the course of the regular rehearsals.

Turning briefly to some of the non-technical considerations which are important to the teacher of instrumental music we are confronted immediately with the question of personality. This somewhat loosely defined term covers a number of elements, any one of which might affect either favorably or adversely the individual teacher's chances of success. All too often discussions on this general subject have avoided such vital matters as physical appearance, taste in dress, grooming and cleanliness, speech habits, disposition, and social qualities in general. The delicacy which has dictated the avoidance of these topics by teachers, authors of textbooks, and others in a position to emphasize their importance has cost many a young teacher his social standing in the community, if not his position in the schools. Those things which "your best friend will not tell you" are so exhaustively elucidated in the current magazine advertisements and over the radio that there is little excuse for their neglect. The difficulty probably rests in the fact that each individual is convinced that all this free advice is intended not for himself, but for someone else.

Self-analysis and a determined effort to correct observed weaknesses cannot fail to contribute largely to the initial success of the beginning teacher or to revitalize the work of many of those already established in the profession. If one is born with an unfortunate profile or an ill-proportioned body, there is little that can be done about it; but skin, hair, and teeth can be made more attractive with care and neatness, and taste in dress can be depended upon to complete an acceptable personal appearance.

In a more exact sense, personality is reflected in the quality of the voice and manner of speaking, in facial expressions, and in one's general attitude in his relations with other people. Since music educators are but a cross-section of humanity, all types of personality will be found in the classrooms of our schools. All too often, the teacher adopts a severity of manner and voice which is both unnecessary and ineffectual and which is badly out of keeping with a subject matter which is designed to reveal esthetic values. At the opposite pole is the teacher whose failure to assert his or her leadership may be traced to a spiritless, apologetic attitude, an inadequate voice, and a generally timid approach which cannot fail to be reflected in the response, or lack of response, of the students. To both of these extreme types of teachers, the obvious suggestions would be that they cultivate a resonant, articulate manner of speaking, keeping the voice as natural as possible even under the confusing and disturbing conditions which sometimes prevail in a classroom (particularly in an instrumental rehearsal); that their manner reflect, so far as possible, a vital interest in the subject being taught and the reactions of the students to the subject matter; and most important of all, that their whole attitude be friendly and agreeable at all times. To achieve these ideals, especially the last, the teacher may find it necessary to re-examine his own philosophy as it bears upon the subject he is teaching and his relationships with his students. The voice, the facial expression, and the attitude are but reflections of the teacher's own thought processes; and if those are negative, disinterested, or distorted, their true nature can hardly be hidden from the sharp eyes and the quick, discerning minds of young students.

This question of the personal approach has been dealt with at some length, first, because it so vitally affects the success of the teacher and consequently the interest and growth of the students, and second, because these personality factors are so closely intertwined with the technical process of teaching that the two are practically inseparable parts of the whole. The explanation of a particularly obscure or subtle problem of instrumental technique, time, tempo, or interpretation might depend almost wholly for its success upon the clarity with which the teacher presents the problem, or even upon his mood, facial expression, or some purely personal device in the form of a nod of the head or a movement of the hand. Just so delicate is the balance when we are dealing with a subject which is based upon science and mathematics but which gains its true significance from its variable elements — a subject in which moods and variations are quite as important as the more exact and mensurable qualities of factual analysis and controlled movement.

Assuming that the teacher possesses all, or most, of the essential qualifications necessary to the pursuit of a successful career — adequate technical training, sound musicianship, teaching skill, a broad knowledge of the instruments, a good personality, and native intelligence — it will seldom be found that these qualifications are present in any individual in complete balance. One will be a better musician than he is a teacher, another will have excellent personal qualities and be an exceptional teacher but not possess an adequate background of technical training and musicianship. Wherever these qualities in the teacher approach a balance we are apt to find a successful teacher at the particular level for which that individual is fitted. Perhaps the most unfortunate situations are those, all too frequently observed, in which a superior talent in one direction is nullified by a glaring lack in another. Perhaps the most common example of this conflict of strength and weakness is that in which musicianship and high artistic ideals are thwarted by a lack of personality, teaching technique, and classroom discipline.

Most teachers succeed, after a fashion, in spite of one or more types of professional deficiency, because they have learned the lesson of adaptation to the particular situation in which they find themselves; and, it must be emphasized, this principle is of the utmost importance. A teacher schooled to the very highest musical and professional standards might conceivably find himself teaching in a community which was not ready for leadership at this high level. In effect such a teacher would be in precisely the same position as the poorly prepared teacher who might find himself suddenly thrust into a situation in which the very highest type of work had become a tradition. In the first instance some degree of adaptation is possible; in the second, the teacher is clearly not equal to the demands of the position. This principle of adaptation applies with equal force to such personal considerations as dress, speech, and mannerism, but in these matters no serious difficulties will be encountered if the teacher will but avoid the extremes. The application of the old precept "Moderation in all things" will usually solve any problems which may arise to plague the new teacher in a strange community.

The somewhat detailed treatment accorded here to the subject of the teacher's qualifications, both personal and professional, seems to be justified by the feeling of inadequacy expressed by many instrumental teachers, by occasional dissatisfaction on the part of school administrators with the work of their teachers, and by an unbiased evaluation of the musical product of the average school system. True, some schools have achieved almost professional competence in performance, both technically and musically, and many of these schools have maintained a high standard year after year; but this only proves what is possible under good leadership aided by administrative understanding and cooperation. The schools which suffer from frequent changes of leadership due to incompetence of one sort or another may be listed as educational and artistic casualties. By a more searching inquiry into those factors of training, personality, and adaptability which may be regarded as fundamental to success in the teaching field, it is hoped that the large group of shifting, ill-adjusted, but willing and courageous instrumental music teachers might be helped toward a greater professional stability. All this is but a prelude to the more detailed study of technical ways and means of developing better orchestras and bands, but consideration of methods must always be regarded as of secondary importance to those more basic issues which have to do with the teacher's personal and artistic qualifications. Small teaching skills can be acquired, methods of organization can be learned, lists of suitable materials can be obtained, and the technique of the various instruments can even be mastered; but there is no satisfactory substitute for a pleasing personality, a sound educational philosophy, or the artistic impulses of the true musician.

CHAPTER II

Professional Conductor or Music Educator?

Most musicians have at one time or another harbored the thought that they might one day become great conductors. The thought of standing before a body of skilled performers and directing them in concert has always held somewhat the same place in the day-dreams of the youthful musician as the picture that must have come to the young professional soldiers of olden days — a picture of gallant leadership in the face of danger, victories won over tremendous odds, the plaudits of victorious armies, and the gratitude of a people. This is the spirit of adventure and of achievement that keeps the world moving; and the striving for position and public acclaim is just as strong among musicians as among soldiers, statesmen, authors, and ordinary business and professional men. In fact, this desire to achieve some measure of distinction is a fundamental human urge and it accounts for many of our everyday decisions and acts.

Our leading orchestra conductors are probably men who have set some such goal for themselves quite early in life and who have held to their objective against all odds until such time as good fortune and special fitness should make a place for them. But for every ambitious conductor who reaches the heights there are many others who are forced by circumstances to occupy a lower rung on the ladder of success; and while the view may be better at the top of the ladder, the footing is likely to be somewhat more secure nearer the ground. Especially is this fact true of those who have not been trained to withstand the higher altitudes of conductorial accomplishments.

This ambition to conduct is in itself commendable, and the school music program has provided an outlet and a training ground for thousands of young musicians who have found in conducting their one means of self-expression and their only real artistic satisfaction. The schools of this country have, in fact, fulfilled the same function as the city and state orchestras and operas and the military bands of

Europe in the training of musicians and conductors. Many of our best young conductors are the products of the schools.

The directorship of one of the larger and more capable school orchestras or bands provides an unusual opportunity for the young conductor who is seeking practical experience, but he should always place the progress of his students before his own professional ambitions. Failure to do so will almost surely prove harmful to the members of the organization and will eventually retard the conductor's own advancement. The one factor which will determine whether in a given situation the results will be beneficial or inimical to the best interests of all concerned is the attitude of the conductor or teacher. If he regards himself primarily as a *conductor* and his organization as a laboratory of musical guinea-pigs, only harm can result; but if, on the other hand, he assumes the attitude of the real teacher, the students will grow and develop technically and musically, and he himself will be the principal gainer in the end.

To draw a fine distinction between these two attitudes is difficult chiefly because examples of the more desirable type of *teacher*-conductor are so rare as to be almost non-existent. By far the great majority of those in charge of orchestras and bands fall within the category of the *conductor*-teacher. Most of these would not admit the allegation because they would not recognize clearly the differences between the two types. Possibly the distinction will become more apparent as some of the more detailed instructional and training devices are explained in succeeding chapters of this work, but for the present a few of the most obvious differences may be mentioned.

At the outset one might raise the question of plan and sequence in the presentation of musical material. Is a program of study prepared in advance for the semester or for the school year, or is the choice of material determined entirely by the demands of public performance or the whim of the teacher? Is any attempt made to balance the musical diet of the organization through the inclusion of varied types of compositions representative of different periods, composers, nationalities, and styles? Does the teacher devote any time in the rehearsal to the presentation of facts about the compositions or their composers? Are interesting and informative comments made from time to time which would relate the music to historical or literary episodes? Does the teacher devote regular rehearsal time to actual instruction and guidance in the technique of the various instruments, principally as regards fingering problems and bowing styles for the stringed instruments and breathing and articulation for the woodwinds and brasses? Is the attention of the group called to interesting problems of orchestration and arranging which have a direct bearing upon the ultimate musical result?

One could enumerate such examples of real education through instrumental music at considerable length, but enough instances have been given to suggest that the training of an instrumental group involves much more than the mere "playing through" of innumerable compositions with only such additional drill as is absolutely necessary to keep the group together.

The *conductor*-teacher will be more concerned with taking the group through a large number of compositions, and in pursuing this policy he may not be too much concerned as to the technical limitations of his players. To him the rehearsal presents an opportunity for the enlargement of his conducting repertory; and if the compositions are played well enough to supply him with a fair rhythmic, harmonic, and melodic structure, his personal requirements will have been satisfied. One does not criticize the conductor for the desire to expand his musical vocabulary, but the method which he adopts cannot be condoned in view of the resultant harm which it works upon the students. The remedy is to be found in a compromise under the terms of which the conductor *teaches* his players the technical fundamentals and thus develops their ability to read at sight and interpret as they read. The reading skill of any amateur group can be enormously expanded if the method is sound. The relationships between correct technique, rhythmic accuracy, observation of dynamic and expressional indications, and a quick grasp of the spirit of the compositions played must be stressed at all times. The players will usually respond to the suggestion that all-round competence will make possible the performance of an enlarged repertory.

In this type of approach we find evidence of real teaching skill and a correct attitude toward the entire problem. The over-ambitious *conductor*-teacher would do well to dust off the old adage, "Make haste slowly," and apply it in the rehearsal by making sure that his players have a thorough grasp of technical and musical fundamentals. Supplementary instruction in the form of individual lessons, section rehearsals, or mixed instrumental classes constitutes a highly desirable adjunct to the regular training of the orchestra or band; but in any case a certain amount of actual teaching must be done as a part of the general rehearsal. This is necessary if for no other reason than to coordinate the work of the various sections and to insure that a single concept of performance prevails throughout the entire organization. Only in this way can a sense of unity be built into an instrumental group.

Perfect ensemble is difficult to define in exact terms. It is more than mere unity in attack and release or group accuracy in the treatment of rhythmic patterns. It is more in the nature of a sixth sense which combines the qualities of mental, emotional, and muscular sympathy between the various players and between the players and the conductor.

The psychologists have a word which should be more widely known and understood by instrumental teachers because it helps to explain the amazing technical and musical accomplishments of performers in all branches of music. This word is *empathy* and it refers to that automatic nervous or muscular response which is experienced, for example, by the player when he sees any given sequence of printed notes. He may not even have his instrument in his hands, but he can sense exactly the manner in which the sequence of notes would be played and how the playing of them would feel.

The importance of this matter for instrumentalists rests in the fact that the force and the clarity and accuracy of the response depends upon the extent of the player's mental grasp of the note sequence and the degree to which the performance of the separate acts essential to a proper execution of the sequence has been drilled into the nervous and muscular structure of the player. This explains the necessity for constant drill on small details of execution required in music, or in any art, profession, or sport which depends for success upon highly developed skills. For the same reason the so-called "whole method" of learning advocated by some progressive educators can never be applied in full to the acquisition of skills in musical performance.

To illustrate further the importance of group teaching and drill in rehearsal, it is frequently possible for an individual player to execute a difficult passage with other players where he would be unable to perform the same passage alone. This is partly a matter of the rhythmic force inherent in the group response, to which is added the fact that the individual puts forth his maximum effort when he functions as a part of a group.

The stimulus for technical growth through practice of this sort must be supplied by the teacher, but above all the rehearsal situation must be so organized that the various sections will have frequent opportunities to utilize this method of growth. In the main, it becomes a process of *analysis,* or the breaking down of the whole into its component parts, and *synthesis,* the replacement or combination of these parts to form the complete structure. This method is used extensively in the solution of problems in fields other than music, and under certain conditions no other process will accomplish the same results. In the mastery of the technical and musical complexities of ensemble performance it has become the accepted practice and it forms the basis, with modifications, of the rehearsal procedure of even the finest symphony orchestras. In the amateur group the chief emphasis is upon drill and instruction, but otherwise the system of study is much the same as in the professional organization.

It has been said that the greatest orchestra conductors are the greatest teachers, and in a large measure this is true. Naturally they need give little attention to matters of technic, but who is to say that the teaching of interpretation is any less exacting than the teaching of technic. A great orchestra is great because its membership includes the finest artists, because the conductor possesses unusual musical insight and imagination, and because the conductor is able to bring about absolute unity of purpose and impress upon his men his own ideas of interpretation. The latter requires of him that he be a teacher of the highest order, especially in view of the fact that he is dealing with men who may have lost some of their youthful enthusiasm for playing and for whom the performance of even the world's finest literature may have lost its original glamour. Surely it requires a great teacher to accomplish the best results, to breathe new life into the same old repertory, and to arouse the dormant enthusiasms of blasé and often artistically tired professional musicians.

It is no less important that the conductor of a school organization be first of all a teacher. He faces the problems of developing basic techniques, of translating innumerable musical terms and symbols, of "selling" good music to a generation which is satiated with jazz, of trying to compensate for the poor instruments with which his players are provided, of trying to keep these instruments in a reasonably acceptable state of repair, and of holding the interest of both advanced and beginning players in one organization with music of the same grade of difficulty. This is no task for an ordinary mortal, but perhaps, after all, teachers are not mortal. Certainly no one but a real teacher would have the courage and the resourcefulness to face such a task and carry it through to a successful conclusion.

In the fact of the existence of hundreds of superb school orchestras and bands we find proof of the organizing ability, the musicianship, and the teaching skill of those responsible for their development; but of these qualities of leadership it must be apparent that the *ability to teach* — with enthusiasm, with efficiency, with resourcefulness and imagination — has been the predominant factor in the success of these individuals.

CHAPTER III

Technique of Teaching Instrumental Ensembles

Since the early nineteenth century, when the art of conducting as we know it today came to be recognized as an essential factor in group performance, the subject has challenged the literary skill of music critics, biographers, musicologists, historians, magazine writers, and poets. Each in his own way has endeavored to discover the qualities which a great conductor must possess, what he must know and be able to do, and how he differs from other artists. For the most part, his real character and the art which he practices have been beclouded rather than clarified by the volumes which have been written. On the one hand the conductor has been pictured as a super-being, endowed with powers not possessed by other mortals; while on the other hand, both his skill and his art have been made to appear insignificant, and to him has been assigned the character of the charlatan, the artistic impostor, the clever showman.

The older literature on the subject is more interesting than informative for the reason that much of it was written in support of personal or professional grudges or to glorify one musician or "school" at the expense of another. Even political intrigues, class feeling, and national hatreds have besmirched the record, not only in regard to the leading conductors of the past and present but also with respect to composers and performing artists. To counterbalance the venomous assaults directed against the artistic integrity of certain conductors, their friends and supporters have come forth with equally false and frequently fantastic claims in their behalf.

To know even a few conductors of distinction and to observe their relationships with colleagues and their attitudes toward the players under their direction make it possible for one to revise his conception of conductors as artists and as men. In this process of reevaluation it is soon discovered that both the criticisms of the detractors and the extravagant claims of the literary dilettante are based largely upon erroneous concepts of the art and the artist.

19

Conductors — and here we refer to the conductors of established symphony orchestras — are, for the most part, men of distinct intellectual attainments, sound artistic impulses, and a consuming interest in the world in which they live. These men have travelled widely, they have enjoyed contacts with successful individuals in all fields, and they are usually prodigious readers and profound students. Contrary to common belief, they are good company and easy to meet and to know. To a surprising extent they are informed regarding the progress of music in the schools, and they view this work with sympathetic interest. Besides being sincere artists, these men are astute and skillful artisans. They know their field and they have confidence in their ability to produce the desired results. Perhaps the soundest advice that might be given the young conductor would be that he seek to emulate the best orchestral conductors in both personal and professional matters, remembering always that his work is in a more restricted field and that he is still a teacher and, as such, must adapt himself to the school situation.

In view of the immense volume of instruction and advice that has been published on the purely technical phases of conducting, there is little need for further treatment of this subject. The fundamental principles of time-beating are generally understood in spite of the fact that they are widely disregarded in practice. Score-reading has been explained in considerable detail in a number of published texts, and even more information can be gleaned on this subject from a study of the scores themselves; but here also we find school instrumental conductors commonly avoiding the use of scores and depending instead upon the so-called condensed scores. Problems of instrumentation, likewise, have been treated exhaustively in standard works by authorities in this special field.

The fact that a great wealth of text material on these vitally important subjects is conveniently available to young conductors would seem to remove the last excuse for any failure to understand basic principles. Nevertheless there exists a very grave lack in this respect on the part of many school orchestra and band conductors who possess all of the other essential qualifications for success. Real and lasting attainments cannot be built upon the flimsy pedagogical admonition to "Do as I say, not as I do." The teacher should know his conducting technique, his scores, and his instrumentation, not to mention his harmony and form, his musical biography and history, and his literature.

Very frequently, however, one observes the puzzling spectacle of a conductor who possesses a substantial knowledge of the theory of his art and even unusual skill in the practical aspects of conducting but who, in spite of these attainments, still fails to achieve the desired results. This situation is so common among school orchestra and band conductors as to suggest the possibility that there is another, and perhaps a more important, phase of the technique of conducting than that which relates to mere time-beating and interpretation. If there exists some such hidden element in the conducting art, the unconscious use of which might explain the success of certain conductors, it is reasonable to believe that general improvement would result from its discovery and dissemination.

Let us assume therefore, as the first step in our investigation, that there are certain elements in the handling of the rehearsal situation which are of vital importance in securing the best results. These practices, whatever they may be, must have become habitual to the conductor who succeeds year after year in producing outstanding groups under varied conditions. For him, at least, the devices which he employs may be regarded as specific techniques in conducting or, possibly, techniques in teaching; but for the purposes of this study the fields of teaching and of conducting are inseparable.

In order to isolate and examine these conducting or teaching techniques which, it appears, may prove to be determining factors in the training of instrumentalists in groups, an analysis of the methods employed by the most successful teachers should prove helpful. In this study no item will be regarded as too insignificant for careful consideration since it is a recognized fact that details are often of paramount importance. A discordant element introduced unconsciously into the orchestra or band rehearsal by a novice conductor might prove just as costly in the final performance as would the faulty adjustment of a spark-gap or carburetor in the motor of one's car. On the positive side, any device, procedure, or technique which will save rehearsal time, stimulate the players to greater effort, and thus point the way to a musically adequate final performance may be regarded as a legitimate part of the technique of conducting. This phase of the art is actually of greater importance in the teaching of music in the schools than even such generally accepted essentials as baton technique, score-reading, and instrumentation. Practically no advice or instruction on this subject has been made available to young conductors either in their formal courses or in textbooks and periodicals.

Specific examples of this branch of teaching technique range from elements which touch upon the purely personal qualifications of the teacher to those which might almost be regarded as problems of instrumental technique, or even interpretation. The difficulty in classifying the subject matter may explain, in part, the failure of teacher-training institutions to provide more direct guidance in this field. Possibly the commonly required courses in "practice-teaching" are supposed to include coverage of these important items, and this would imply, in turn, that the supervisor of practice-teaching has organized the subject as a separate unit and has presented it with an emphasis commensurate with its practical importance. This, unfortunately, has not been the case, at least insofar as the great majority of institutions is concerned.

Almost all of the teaching or conducting techniques which fall within the scope of this discussion are directed toward the single purpose of making the most effective use of rehearsal time; and so it seems appropriate to place at the head of the list the teacher's habits of speech. Needless to say, he should cultivate a pleasing voice and manner of speech, but of even greater importance is the fact that every word and every syllable must be heard distinctly by every member of the organization. However, these are preliminary considerations. The vital point is that the teacher must present his ideas or instructions in the briefest possible form and so phrased that the thought is transferred with crystal clarity. In the main, he should present only one or two ideas at a time. A break in the performance or the drill process should be for a specific purpose — to make a correction, to suggest a better technical approach, or to improve the interpretation. Whatever purpose necessitates the halt should be fulfilled quickly and effectively, and the rehearsal should proceed at once. This is a definite teaching technique, and it demands study on the part of the conductor. His thought processes must be well ahead of those of his students; he must detect not only the problem but its best solution in the twinkling of an eye; and he must have his instruction phrased and ready to present as soon as the group ceases playing. Not only will such a method be the means of accomplishing much in a given length of time, but the students will respond to the rehearsal situation with alertness and general interest. Love of activity is one of the strong characteristics of youth, and another which is equally prominent is youth's desire for achievement. Both of these demands will be met by the conductor who cultivates an active, clean-cut approach — who leads the group, not only with the baton but also intellectually and spiritually.

Unfortunately, the factors which make for complete success are too elusive to be isolated and card-indexed. No two conductors are likely to have exactly the same problems; and even in those instances in which their problems might appear to be similar, quite different remedial measures would usually be required. For example, let us assume the existence of two otherwise equally competent conductors, both of whom employ about the same approach in the matter of detailed analysis and drill in rehearsals. One succeeds quite easily in attaining his objectives; the other fails to sustain interest. What are the reasons for this discrepancy in the results obtained? There may be several reasons, including differences in speech habits, manner of presentation, and the like; but a more important basic reason is likely to be that the successful conductor selects truly significant problems for analysis, while the other spends valuable time upon relatively unimportant matters. Or, to cite another possible difference, one may make his explanations meaningful to the entire group while the other may, by his manner, exclude all but a few players from active consideration of the problem at hand. It is just such details as these that often mark the difference between success and failure in teaching and conducting. They are, for the most part, matters of rehearsal organization and teaching technique which are closely interwoven, and which must be developed and perfected in terms of their application to specific problems.

The best results can be obtained only by the "stop and start" method suggested above for the very obvious reason that a group which makes a habit of playing compositions in their entirety without any pauses for correction is in effect *practicing mistakes,* and such an organization will never attain perfection. It has often been stated in this connection that "It is harder to go back than it is to go forward." The conductor should stop the group whenever he feels that a major improvement can be effected unless, of course, the project of the moment happens to be sight-reading practice. The essential need of the "stop and start" technique of operating the rehearsal should be apparent to all, but this raises the question of how to do this without confusion and loss of time. This, again, depends upon the skill of the conductor and upon his ability to dominate the rehearsal situation. In order to command the immediate attention of all, he should play upon the fact that when a stop is signalled no player knows but that the halt is being made on his particular account. Each player will be alert to discover whether he is to be the object of the conductor's attentions. Any difficulty in obtaining a satisfactory response to these sudden stop-signals must be dealt with by each conductor in his own way, but the correct response must be developed if the best results are to be attained. This, again, is but a phase of conducting technique.

Wasting rehearsal time is a crime against the members of the organization, against the taxpayers and the community, and against one's chosen art and profession. If we accept this definition of crime, it must be admitted that a considerable number of conductors of both amateur and professional orchestras and bands must be classified as criminals. Among the principal causes of this widespread habit of time-wasting are poor organization, the partial or complete absence of discipline, and the use of utterly worthless musical material. One less easily detected method of wasting valuable rehearsal time is that of drilling on non-essential items, or items which will be corrected automatically with further practice. To avoid this pitfall the conductor must study his score with a view to discovering those difficulties which are fundamental or which involve some new principle not understood by the players. These special problems should receive attention first, and if time permits, matters of lesser importance may be treated later. The conductor of a professional group frequently finds it necessary, due to the restricted time for rehearsal, to confine his work with the organization entirely to these special problems which he selects in advance. School orchestra and band conductors would do well to adopt this practice, at least in principle.

The analysis of scores, upon which any proper organization of rehearsal procedure must be based, will disclose specific problems which may be regarded primarily as problems of group response and which require for their solution the application of some sort of teaching or drill device evolved or invented for this special purpose. As an example of this type of problem one might cite the following passage:

SYMPHONY No.V IN E MINOR – LARGO – DVORAK (Orchestra)

This is an extremely difficult passage and one that would require long and tedious drill but for the happy circumstance that the sixteenth note figuration is repeated in exactly the same form and with the same tonality by the oboe, clarinet, flute, violins, celli, and basses in the order named. The trill figuration likewise is repeated in turn by some of these instruments. In this case the obvious solution is to have the triplet figure played first by the oboe while the other players study their parts or perhaps finger their instruments silently. Then all should play the measure *in unison* (and octaves, as the case may be). A few slow repetitions of the measure, interspersed with some special instructions regarding the fingering of the string parts, the observance of the accidentals, and the mention of the fact that the clarinet part is legato while all other parts are staccato, and the passage is well advanced toward final mastery. The very same plan is then followed with the second measure containing the trill problem, and finally the entire passage is played as written. This entire process is an invention by which loss of time, wasted effort, and mistakes can be prevented. Each teacher must devise his own solutions as the needs are presented, but in every case the problem must be thoroughly understood before a suitable corrective measure can be applied. Some remedies will be more successful than others, and unless considerable care is exercised there is the possibility that the remedial device will prove more complex than the original problem.

The following excerpt from the Scherzo movement of the same symphony will still further clarify this principle, although the problem here is one which concerns an individual instrument, in this case the violin:

In the absence of specific help on this problem, the section will find it practically unplayable, yet in fact it can be mastered with the right approach and sufficient practice. The following plan is suggested: Practice the first three notes, taking the high C on the A string with the fourth finger. Practice the double-stop interval in the sixth position, emphasizing the close position of the fingers. Add the next two notes in the sequence with the second and first fingers on the A string. The following exercises illustrate these three steps:

Having established the basic pattern, the rhythm, bowing, and trill can be developed without much difficulty. For the next two measures the very same technique applies in the third position, the secret of the entire sequence being the double-stop conception of the finger positions. A variety of different fingerings and positions may be used, but the double-stop method of playing the interval of a sixth must always be employed for the best results.

Similar difficulties exist in the parts for all instruments. The trombone part of an orchestral or band composition, for example, might contain such a passage as the following:

The slide positions indicated above the notes are the usual positions (the only ones which many young players know), while those below the notes are the alternate positions. Even this short passage might be played in several different ways. Using both regular and alternate positions in various sequences, the advanced player would be able to play the passage in a variety of styles ranging from extreme facility in execution or maximum power to a smooth, singing legato. The wrong choice of position sequences might seriously impair the quality of the performance even for a skillful player. This same principle applies in the case of all of the valve brass instruments.

One of many possible examples of fingering simplifications as it applies to the clarinet is the following:

Normally the B-flat is played by the first and second fingers of the left hand with the third finger pressing the B-flat key or the first finger of the right hand pressing a side key which serves the same function. This note can also be played by the first finger of each hand covering open holes, and by using this fingering the change from the F to the B-flat can be executed simply by lifting the second and third fingers of the left hand. A like simplification is possible between the D and the B-flat in the latter half of the measure. The added facility with which these sequences can be played by the use of the substitute fingerings must be experienced or observed to be fully appreciated.

Because of the limitations of space and the practically inexhaustible dimensions of this problem of simplification through use of the correct fingering combination, slide position, or position sequence, only three simple examples have been given by way of illustration. It is one of the major responsibilities of the conductor, however, to know the more common of these technical solutions and to be able to apply his knowledge in rehearsal before valuable time has been wasted in attempting to master passages which would be practically unplayable by the methods which the student would normally employ.

One of the most valuable phases of orchestral and band training is the general knowledge of instruments and instrumentation which comes to the players quite naturally if the music is properly presented. In the beginning the instrumental ensemble may impress the young player who is just entering the group as a gigantic hodgepodge of sound. Gradually, as he commences to adjust to his surroundings, he begins to distinguish certain of the more prominent voices. This growth in comprehension is, of course, more marked in the beginning, and sometimes it is arrested completely just as the problem begins to assume real interest. If this occurs the fault is that of the conductor for his failure to build upon the natural curiosity of the student and incorporate into the general program of instruction a more or less systematic study of instrumentation. This does not imply that he should substitute this for the routine work of the rehearsal, but that he adopt certain practices which would serve both ends simultaneously. The obvious facts about the various groups of instruments will develop from the manner in which the parts are treated in ensemble writing. The string family, the reed family, the brass family, and the percussion instruments will be readily isolated; but it is the next step in the process which calls for some special attention by the conductor. For example, he should make special mention of any unusual combination of instruments or treatment of any given part. He might find occasion to show, by contrast, some of the various possibilities in the way of instrumentation. It might be necessary for him to reinforce a certain part by having another instrument play "cues," or a special part might have to be written for this purpose. The players should be told the reasons for such

changes. An even more effective method of extending the players'
knowledge of other instruments and their possibilities in combination
is by drilling on certain difficult passages in unusual and even remote
combinations — the oboe, string bass, and horns, for example; the
violins and the low brasses; or in the band, a combination of flutes,
saxophones, and solo cornet. The use of such odd combinations does
two things: it places an extra responsibility upon the players in the
matter of counting, articulation, general coordination, and timing;
and it demonstrates clearly to them the importance of writing for
the *proper* combination of instruments in the correct balance and
proportion.

An unnatural voicing will not only produce poor tonal results
but will add greatly to the difficulty of controlling and blending the
parts in matters of intonation and balance. The following chord
sequence from a well-known composition for band will serve to illustrate this point:

The difficulty of obtaining satisfactory results from this combination and spacing of instruments can be appreciated only by hearing the passage played. The mixture of bassoon, saxophone, and bass
tone on the low F of the first chord, bassoon and bass clarinet on the
C, and horn and tenor saxophone on the F above is sufficient to rob
the chord of any characteristic quality. The F, played in three octaves by instruments of totally different quality, can be neither
blended nor played in tune. To make matters still worse, the clarinet
is assigned its B-flat, a tone which is out-of-tune and of poor quality
on most instruments. The combination of instruments used in the
second chord — E-flat clarinet (also assigned to the defective throat
tone A), clarinet, and alto clarinet with alto saxophone in supposed
unison — could not fail to produce the worst possible effect. It should

be observed also that there are no tones in common between the two chords, no instruments in common, and the total range varies from three octaves to slightly more than one octave. The players themselves will recognize that there is a deficiency in the arrangement, but it will remain for the conductor to utilize this and similar problems as a means of teaching the group something about the basic principles of arranging. This passage might be rearranged in several different forms; and it would probably be improved by a better harmonic distribution of both chords, but this is hardly permissible. After such passages have been rewritten the two versions should be compared in the laboratory of actual performance. One suggested revision is the following:

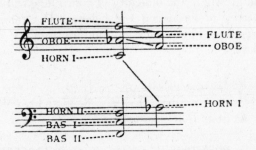

The effect would be further improved by sustaining the bassoon and second horn parts into the third beat.

In most instrumental organizations too little attention is given to problems of attack and release. This is an element which is seldom emphasized in the ordinary course in conducting. There are many different types of attack, depending upon the mood of the composition or of its various parts, the arrangement of the chords, the tempo, the dynamic level, and other factors. These various attacks range from the sharpest conceivable "prepared" attack in the upper dynamic levels to a starting tone which can hardly be said to have any beginning, so gently and gradually does it float into the consciousness of the listener. There is a specific technique for producing these different attacks on the various instruments, but this is a question which will be treated in some detail in a later chapter.

There are three vitally important points concerning the question of attack which must be emphasized; first, that the appropriate type or style of attack must be employed; second, that the attack must be absolutely unified; and third, that in order to attain the desired perfection the attack must be practiced as such. The achievement of even a fair degree of success under the first item involves careful and analytical repetition and experimentation in order to develop in the individual players the necessary control of bow pressure and speed, or embouchure and breath pressure. Attention to these items will tend to make the performers more sensitive to small errors in execution and more conscious of the real significance of good ensemble. Lack of unity in attack is traceable either to inattention on the part of the players or inexactness in the conductor's beat. There must be a natural and consistent preparatory movement of the baton and a sharp focus on the "point" of the beat which signals the attack. Finally, the attack should be practiced with sufficient frequency to insure satisfactory results. In brief, the perfect attack should become a habit and an inviolable rule of performance if for no other reason than that it produces a correct psychological set for all that follows. The attack should be practiced on single chords only, and the temptation to go on to irrelevant material in succeeding measures should be resisted.

All that has been said about the attack applies with equal force to the matter of release. The release should conform to the nature of the final chord or the passage under consideration. Definite practice to achieve unity of release is of the utmost importance. In work with amateur groups the "circular" release has been found most effective. This technique involves the delineation of a complete clockwise circle with the baton, either large or small depending upon the dynamic level of the final chord or the amount of preparatory notice desired. The rule is a simple one for the student to understand: Release the tone when the baton returns to its starting point. The stroke is usually started and ended at the bottom of the circle. The common disregard for the necessity of providing this preparatory baton stroke accounts for much of the careless release which distinguishes the work of many professional and amateur groups.

High on any list of the important items in group training should be those which have to do with increasing the rhythmic accuracy or intensity of the performance. Amateur organizations are the worst offenders in this category. The "sing-song" manner in which many such groups play may be traced to several different factors, including lack of dynamic contrast, rhythmic inaccuracies, disregard of bowings and articulations, and faulty intonation; but the chief cause of this common weakness is the almost total absence of metrical and rhythmic accentuation. The teaching techniques which are required to remedy this situation must be based upon the general idea of inducing, at first, a greatly exaggerated pulsation. A basic consideration here is the question of the technique of pulsation — for the winds a stronger attack on the accented beats through the use of the breath, and for the strings an elastic pressure exerted on the bow by the fingers, wrist, and forearm. But the main goal should be to make the players more conscious of the value of pulsation, and for this purpose no device has proved more effective than the comparison of the music to the human body. If the heart-beat — the pulse — is weak and irregular, the person is ill; if the beating of the pulse stops entirely, the person is dead. The same truths apply to the musical pulse, and the results are equally inconvenient or fatal, as the case may be. The advantages of a strong and regular musical pulse are observed chiefly in a more interesting performance and one which reflects the special character of the music being played, but there is an added gain for amateurs in the fact that a good pulse makes it easier for the group to keep together and to maintain the correct tempo.

The importance of pulsation as such should not be permitted to obscure the fact that relative note-values are the true basis of rhythm. The appropriate degree of pulsation will improve the effect of a correctly-played rhythmic pattern, and it may even help the player achieve a more accurate interpretation of the note-values which are indicated; but there must always be the proper mental conception of the rhythm groups and their relationship to the basic meter and tempo. Rhythmic patterns should be regarded as definite objects, the distinctive features of which must be learned by the music student in much the same way that a young child gradually acquires an awareness of various household articles and learns to identify them. Each rhythm has its own special characteristics, and the speed and accuracy with which identification is made will determine the rhythmic aptitude of the player. First must come recognition — clear and unmistakable; then application of the principle of intensive pulsation within the limitations imposed by the musical character of the passage being studied.

A very practical teaching device is the use in simple scale form of such difficult rhythmic patterns as may be encountered in the course of the rehearsal. The following examples will illustrate the method of application:

Example: MARCH FROM "LOVE OF THREE ORANGES"—PROKOFIEFF

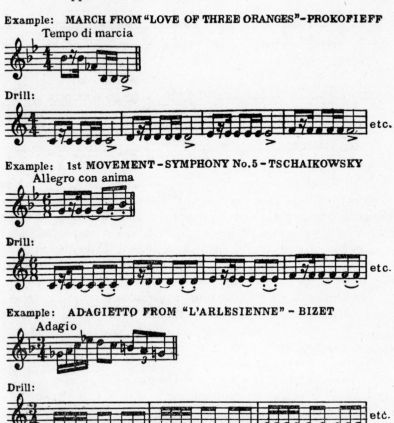

The rhythmic patterns employed should be taken directly from the compositions which are being studied, as in this way the drill has a definite purpose in the eyes of the students. In each case the basic pattern should be indicated on a blackboard in order that the connection between notation, rhythmic response, and muscular movement be firmly established. This type of study can sometimes be made effective by asking the students to tap the rhythms before attempting to play them.

Rhythmic patterns involving rests sometimes present almost insurmountable obstacles, especially if a short rest falls upon a normally accented beat and if it is followed by a succession of notes of short duration. The following examples will illustrate the problem:

In both of these instances there is an almost irresistible impulse to delay the entrance and then to accent the note following the rest. The remedy is found in "filling in" the rests with notes for purposes of drill and in exaggerating the natural accents. Once the student appreciates that a strong accent must fall upon the fourth note in the sequence (as written), he will be able to play the passage correctly. This leads to the statement of a teaching principle which merits frequent repetition, namely, that if the accents are placed upon the right notes, there will be very little chance of playing the rhythmic pattern incorrectly.

Intonation is the one problem for which no permanent solution has as yet been found. It is a continual source of annoyance, uncertainty, and sometimes an approach perilously near to artistic disaster; but there are encouraging signs in the discovery of certain tuning techniques. These are time-consuming devices, but there is comfort in the knowledge that any rehearsal time devoted to tuning of the proper sort will prove helpful in developing other vitally important elements in performance. Chief among these subsidiary gains from tuning practice are: first, concentration on all types of pitch problems, which carries over into performance; second, appreciation of subtle differences in tone quality and dynamics; and third, balance within and between sections of the organization. Since the general problem of intonation is of such scope and importance as to require a more detailed exposition than is convenient at this point, a later chapter will deal exclusively with the subject. There are certain fundamental principles, however, which come logically under the heading of teaching techniques. These are stated briefly in the order of their importance.

Each player should be expected to produce in correct pitch, i.e., as the tone sounds, any note the conductor might name. This involves a limited knowledge of transposition, at least as it applies to the player's own instrument. As the conductor names a succession of single notes, the group responds with the appropriate pitch, sounding in unisons and octaves. This provides a basis for the preliminary, or "rough" tuning. By naming simple triads the conductor advances to the next step in the tuning process, and finally he calls for seventh chords and more complicated harmonic progressions. Throughout this type of unison and chord tuning the group must, at first, be admonished to play softly and to observe a satisfactory dynamic balance between parts. This system of tuning is based upon the theory of the necessity for instantaneous pitch adjustment to the predominant chord structure; and its ultimate success must rest upon the alertness of the group, its sensitiveness to small differences in pitch, and above all, cooperation in the general project of pitch improvement.

Closely related to the matter of intonation is that of recognizing the distinctive tonality of chords. Ordinarily this presents no difficulties, especially if the chords are constructed of simple diatonic combinations and if they are in the more usual positions and instrumental combinations. On occasion, however, one encounters a harmony which the student-players seem unable to grasp, even after repeated trials. These chords are usually of a dissonant structure and even when they are played correctly the result is at first displeasing to ears accustomed to the more obvious harmonies. As a direct result of this reaction the students seem temporarily incapable of making the necessary pitch adjustments and dynamic modifications which would reveal the true character of the chord. For this situation three possible remedies are suggested. First, have the chord sounded by sections and then by the entire group. If this fails to produce the desired result, name the notes of the chord in order and ask the entire organization to play each of the notes named in unison as described in the preceding paragraph. This should establish the tonality, but if it does not, the conductor should as a last resort, fall back upon that great American "crutch" — the piano. After hearing the harmony played once or twice the orchestra or band should have little difficulty in producing a satisfactory chord. The conductor should always be alert, of course, to discover misprints in the music or simple errors in note-reading which might account for the failure of the group as a whole to discover the correct harmony.

The limited use of the piano referred to above raises the issue of its proper place in the orchestra or band rehearsal. In principle, the teaching of instrumental music by rote methods presents a faulty and destructive concept, but it must be recognized that the piano has a legitimate place in the teaching of both orchestras and bands. The demonstration of a musical idea or a rhythmic pattern on the piano may be more effective than any amount of verbal analysis or any number of unsuccessful attempts on the part of the group to produce the correct result. This method saves time and may, if the conductor possesses the requisite pianistic facility, greatly enlarge the musical understanding of the players. Another element which would seem to justify the moderate extension of this practice is that the students seem to enjoy the small diversion which it supplies through the introduction of a new tone color. When the piano is used with the orchestra or band, the players invariably react to the performance with a new interest. In passing, it should be pointed out that the condensed scores usually provided with both orchestra and band arrangements constitute a suitable piano part for use in this connection.

Many conductors and teachers seem not to appreciate the fact that the piano is not, strictly speaking, a regular orchestral instrument. Its use, except as suggested in the preceding paragraph, should normally be limited to supplying missing parts in very small or poorly balanced ensembles or as a solo instrument for which the orchestra (or band) supplies an accompanying or equal part. An orchestra, for example, which embodies a complete, or nearly complete, instrumentation should never make use of the piano in either rehearsals or concerts except as suggested above. The instrument merely "doubles" parts which are much more interesting and beautiful in their own tone coloring and technical idiom. It is impossible to obtain any real blend or sympathy between the percussive quality of the piano and the smoother, more liquid character of the flute, the horn, or the clarinet. In fact, even in incomplete orchestras (or bands) it would be far more desirable to provide the missing parts through the medium of a reed organ than by means of the piano. The single exception might be the substitution or the reenforcement of certain types of string bass parts on the piano.

The use of the piano as a teaching aid places a new emphasis upon the importance of every young conductor's learning to play this instrument, at least sufficiently well to enable him to demonstrate essential basic patterns and harmonies. The same applies to other instruments of the orchestra and band. The school instrumental program has progressed to a stage of advancement which demands of its leadership the ability to play exceedingly well upon one major instrument and sufficiently well for purposes of demonstration upon several other instruments of different types. A minimum of theoretical knowledge and practical playing skill might suffice for a limited time or in a small teaching situation, but an exacting leadership demands much more than this. Words of advice and instruction suddenly assume real force when the conductor is able to take over the player's own instrument and demonstrate clearly and unmistakably how a given passage should be played. Of greatest value to the conductor of the orchestra is the ability to play the violin or the cello, whereas the band conductor will serve his organization best if he is a skilled executant on one of the principal woodwind instruments, preferably the clarinet. The broader the scope of the conductor's performing skill the better will be the results he is able to attain; but in no case can he afford to be without a comprehensive and practical knowledge of the construction, fingering, and technique of all of the instruments which he may be called upon to teach.

The drill technique of having certain sections, or combinations of sections, perform given passages has already been discussed, and the importance of this procedure cannot be overemphasized. In fact, a very considerable portion of every rehearsal might well be given over to this type of analysis and drill. Of equal importance, however, is the device of still further breaking down the performance to the point of asking individual students to play short passages in rotation. This is the only method by which the conductor can know with certainty what goes on behind the full ensemble and what corrective measures are necessary in individual cases. Furthermore, this practice multiplies a hundred-fold the player's own sense of his responsibility to the organization, and the total gain in attitude and performance far outweighs the cost of the procedure in time and effort.

For those teachers who have never applied this technique a word of advice and warning is in order. Young pupils are extremely proud and sensitive, especially in the presence of their fellows, and for this reason the process of individual drill must be handled with the utmost delicacy. A general air of ease, good-will, and good humor must prevail, and it should be made clear to all that mistakes — serious mistakes — are expected, and that no great calamity will befall those who perpetrate these errors. All are "in the same boat" and trying to reach the shore of technical and artistic achievement together. This is merely a means of learning from one another. One will excel in a given category — tone, technique, intonation, interpretation, rhythmic accuracy, posture, manner of holding the instrument — whereas another will establish a higher standard in a different branch of performance. The teacher should be extremely liberal with his encouragement, but he should likewise inject constructive advice in a manner which suggests that all in the group require the same correction as that called forth by the individual performance. Grave faults must be passed over lightly, to be discussed later with the individual in strict privacy. Very sensitive or nervous students might be "accidentally" overlooked until the group becomes more used to the individual tests and drills. In this method will be found one of the most valuable of all technical devices and its chief value rests in the fact that no student knows with certainty when he may be called upon to play a given passage alone. The mild threat which always hangs over his head causes him to practice somewhat more than he otherwise might, and certainly with greater purpose and more attention to technical and musical fundamentals than would otherwise be the case.

The conductor must exert some care in the matter of interspersing this individual drill throughout the rehearsal in such manner that the group does not lose interest in the main activity, which is the general performance of the entire group. It is impossible to say what proportion of time should be allocated to full ensemble playing, sectional drill, and work with individuals, as this will depend somewhat upon the skill of the director, the willingness of the players to accept a teaching process which might be more beneficial but less interesting, and perhaps, upon the type of music being performed and the advancement of the group. In any event, the conductor who uses the individual method extensively should distribute his attentions throughout all sections in order to keep all members of the orchestra or band alert and to forestall any disciplinary problems which might arise from inactivity. The success of this device, it might be added, will depend almost entirely upon the ability of the conductor to make his suggestions interesting and applicable to all members of the group.

In much of what has already been said regarding the various drill devices there is the suggestion that the "breaking-down" process should be applied not only to the instrumentation but to the music itself. If it is necessary or desirable to hear sections in combination and alone, and even at times individual players, it is equally important that smaller and still smaller portions of the music be made the unit of study. The reason for this is obvious. The correct approach to the mastery of any activity which requires a high degree of proficiency in the execution of a large number of unit skills, is to treat these skills separately at first, then gradually to combine and coordinate them. Ideally, the orchestra or band player might be expected to acquire the requisite skills before becoming a member of a performing organization, but in a school situation this is not often possible. Even if it were possible in the case of the individual, there still remains the problem of cultivating the group skills.

The conductor's task is always to bring the weaker elements in his organization up to the level of the stronger, and this is a continuous process. Regardless of the previous training of the individuals, new faults will appear from time to time, and these must be treated by much the same method as that employed by the football coach. If his squad begins to show inadequacies in blocking, mastery of signals, or ball-handling, he concentrates upon these specific problems until some improvement is shown. If the band conductor suddenly becomes aware of general carelessness in intonation, articulation, or group tone quality, he selects as a basis for special drill such passages as tend to emphasize these essentials. So the general problem may be viewed as a continuing series of corrective and developing techniques calculated to retain the elements of strength and to eliminate the more serious weaknesses. This is accomplished best by selecting for special drill, short phrases, single measures, or even smaller groups of notes which embody the germ of a musical idea or a technical problem. If the basic problem is properly presented, one or two repetitions will usually suffice to establish the correct form.

Even some of our leading symphony orchestra conductors have made the mistake of placing too great an emphasis upon detail and too little upon the coordination of the various elements into a comprehensive whole. A final performance must be so thoroughly integrated that one part blends with another to form a complete musical idea. This broader concept cannot be achieved without a careful interlocking of such units as may have been subjected to dissection and microscopic analysis in the early rehearsals. The listening audience will not hear the composition as a complete art work having width, height, depth, and proportion unless the players have first viewed it with this broader perspective. Gradually, the more fragmentary concept which is an essential condition of technical mastery must give way to a more comprehensive treatment. When, and under what conditions, this transfer of emphasis is achieved will depend upon many factors applicable only to the particular situation, but the problem will be recognized as one of the difficult-to-classify techniques of conducting.

The discussion of this general subject would not be complete without at least a casual mention of a number of techniques which combine definite mechanical and musical gain with an element of fun for the players and, possibly, relaxation for the conductor.

One such device, used most effectively in connection with a composition which calls for frequent but not parallel periods of rest for the various sections, involves the counting aloud of all of these rest periods. All parts are played, of course, but only as a sort of musical background to ensemble counting. The cornet section starts the usual pattern: *One* – two, *Two* – two, *Three* – two, *Four* – two, etc., and somewhere in the sequence other sections come in with *their: One* – two, *Two* – two, etc. It is frankly a game, but it works out well in making a fixed habit of counting; and failure in this regard, most conductors will agree, is one of the major weaknesses of amateur ensemble playing.

Another similar procedure is to ask the members of certain sections to sing their parts, using some neutral syllable as a basis. Care must be exercised that the composition selected for the purpose is in a slow-moving four-part style well within the range limits of the voices. Some experiments have even been conducted with strictly instrumental idioms in which the players have found it necessary to raise or lower the parts in the octave to keep them within the vocal range. These trials have been fairly successful and have usually resulted in a more legato playing style. Instrumentalists and instrumental teachers are frequently oblivious to the close link between voices and instruments. Most music is based in part upon the vocal style. All wind instrument players utilize almost the same breathing technique as does the singer, and even the strings and the voice have much in common. The oft-repeated truth, "If you cannot sing it, you cannot play it," deserves careful consideration on the part of all instrumentalists. Certain obvious qualifications must be applied, but at least the instrumentalist must have the same mental and emotional conception of melodic material as is demanded of the singer. To make the picture complete, every band and orchestra player should be urged and entreated to gain as much choral experience as possible.

Simple drills in transposition by the entire ensemble provide an interesting and at the same time constructive activity. This practice should also be applied to slower and easier numbers at first, and the key differentials should be very elementary in the beginning. This type of activity should not be given any great amount of rehearsal time, but its occasional introduction will at least emphasize in the minds of the players the importance of their recognizing the common musical intervals and of their having a good working knowledge of key relationships.

In the serious business of learning the technique of the instruments and the elements of notation, many young players and even older musicians have lost sight of the fact that playing for fun also has its place in the realm of music. How many of our school orchestra and band members ever play "by ear" tunes which they may have heard, and how many of them ever attempt to make their own tunes? Our highly organized music program has left little place for this sort of free musical impulse. As an experiment in the cultivation of natural music, "faking," or improvisation, the device of having the entire orchestra or band play, without music, such tunes as *Chop-sticks*, *London Bridge*, or *Old Black Joe* will pay large dividends in unsuspected directions. The players should be advised to play, if they can, idiomatic parts for their instruments. For example, the basses should play a straight tonic, subdominant, dominant sequence; the horns a rhythmic-harmonic part; celli or baritones a counter-melody; and so forth. The conductor should not be surprised if, at first, the basses attempt to play the lead melody, but he and they will learn some interesting facts about the natural ability, or lack of it, possessed by our school musicians. As greater skill in this musical game is acquired, it will be found interesting to develop variations on the themes, counter-melodies, and even a few trick harmonies. This program is not suggested for serious consideration, but only to show to what lengths the creation of special devices and techniques may be carried in the building of mechanical skills and musical insight. Each teacher will develop his own techniques, his own formulas for achieving the desired results, and to a very considerable extent his success will depend upon the effectiveness of the devices and procedures themselves and upon the enthusiasm and force with which the teacher presents them. Foresight and imagination are, after all, factors of supreme importance in any branch of the teaching profession.

CHAPTER IV

Organization of the Rehearsal

The first matter that comes to our attention when we think of rehearsal organization is the type of room or hall in which the rehearsal is held. Its size, proportions, interior finish, lighting, ventilation, furnishings, and location may all have an important bearing upon the organization of the rehearsal and the ultimate achievements of the orchestra or band. It cannot be said that proper housing is the one determining factor between success and failure for the very obvious reason that some of the finest organizations have been produced under the worst conceivable physical handicaps. The training of an instrumental organization is far too complex a matter to be governed entirely by external conditions. Other things being equal, however, a rehearsal hall which is reasonably satisfactory in all essential respects should contribute largely, if not to the artistic growth of the orchestra or band, then at least to the enjoyment of the rehearsal hour and the personal satisfaction of the teacher.

Probably the great majority of school instrumental groups are housed in partially or wholly unsuitable quarters. When the rehearsal space is not the auditorium stage, it is either the gymnasium or a converted classroom which can lay claim to any disadvantages not already preempted by the first two. It is needless to discuss these disadvantages in detail, but an enumeration of them might be the means of improving a situation which must surely be a common cause of at least partial failure. A few of the drawbacks of such rehearsal areas have already been suggested — poor lighting, inadequate temperature control and ventilation, limited and badly-proportioned space, wholly unsuitable furnishings, and poor location. The writer has taught instrumental classes regularly in school furnace rooms, domestic science kitchens, woodwork shops, classrooms fitted with old-style fixed desks, corridors, and school attics, not to mention auditorium stages partially filled with scenery and stage properties, and school gymnasiums. To offset this drab picture there have been

45

a few of the most modern rehearsal halls, fully equipped with every desired convenience and aid to teaching. Such magnificent accommodations as one finds on occasion in the more modern schools are in sharp contrast with the spectacle (an actual case) of an orchestra rehearsal being conducted in one end of a school gymnasium while a basketball practice session is in progress at the far end!

A proper rehearsal room should provide adequate floor space (risers or flat surface) to accommodate the largest of the school's instrumental organizations without crowding. In addition to the area actually required by the organizations, the rehearsal room should contain at least an equal amount of free space to accommodate various items of equipment and to provide for adequate resonance. High ceilings and good lighting are also important factors. If there are not properly curtained windows on two, or preferably three, sides of the room, this lighting deficiency and its improper distribution should be corrected by the installation of indirect or screened overhead lights. For the protection of instruments and the efficiency of the players the temperature should be reasonably constant at 68° to 72°. Adequate storage space for both school owned and privately owned instruments should be provided either within the rehearsal hall or in an adjoining smaller room. In the latter case several wide entrances and exits must be provided to prevent crowding and consequent damage to instruments. A sufficient number of adjustable, but not the light folding type, music stands and straight-back chairs should be permanently in place within the area used for rehearsal. Players should not in any case be expected to transport or arrange the furniture required for the rehearsal as this tires the players unnecessarily, takes time which should be devoted to practice, and creates an atmosphere of confusion which is inimical to the best interests of any musical organization. Proper storage space for the music library should also be conveniently available, and the conductor should be provided with office space adjoining the rehearsal room, or at least an area within the hall screened off for such use.

The above brief outline of the physical requirements of the school orchestra or band represent a reasonable minimum. Beyond this there is no fixed limit. The addition of small practice rooms, storage space for uniforms and special equipment, and a small shop for repairs and the mending of music have become increasingly common with the growth of the music program.

Assuming the availability of more or less satisfactory housing and rehearsal equipment, the question of the number, length, and distribution of rehearsal periods assumes importance. In general, there is little uniformity of procedure even among schools of the same size and employing the same type of scholastic program. The more progressive schools have long maintained daily rehearsals of from forty to eighty minutes for each major group, and the minimum time allowance for any degree of constructive work is usually set at three one-hour rehearsals each week, preferably on alternate days. Many schools find it necessary to get along with even fewer rehearsals. A comprehensive program of instrumental training should probably provide additional periods for individual or group instruction and perhaps some opportunity for selected students to rehearse in small ensembles, but it should be remembered that normal boys and girls have many and varied interests in and out of school. The music program is entitled only to a fair and reasonable share of the student's time and interest regardless of the demands of contest work, special concerts, and the conductor's personal ambition to operate a symphony orchestra or a concert band of near-professional accomplishments.

For the protection of the conductor and the organization, and as a means of insuring the same type of regular and systematic instruction as is expected in academic courses, the school administration should control the number, frequency, and nature of all public appearances. Unless performances are strictly limited to, at most, one each month, the conductor will find it impossible to do any constructive teaching. Organizations which have been under pressure from the public to provide entertainment more or less indiscriminately and without adequate advance notice might find it desirable to establish a fixed policy in this regard. An administration which has a correct attitude toward education as such will usually be more than willing to cooperate with the band and orchestra conductor in effecting a permanent solution of this problem. The mechanics of the situation are quite simple. Written applications should be filed with the school principal at least three weeks before the proposed engagement, these applications to be acted upon by a "committee." In practice, the conductor's recommendation should be accepted; but if it is inconvenient to comply with the request, or if questions of politics or policy make compliance inadvisable, the conductor will then be adequately protected by the administration, as he should be in all such cases.

The subjects which have been discussed in the preceding paragraphs are as closely connected with rehearsal organization as are any questions which might arise in the rehearsal itself because they have a direct bearing upon the progress of the group and the attainment of its immediate and its ultimate objectives. In this same category are the matters of rehearsal "set-up," music distribution, and attendance checking. As suggested previously, an adequate supply of chairs and stands must be available in the rehearsal hall. These chairs and stands should, if possible, be arranged in definite order before the actual time of the rehearsal. Arrangements might be made to have this done by the school janitor or possibly by a student, but in any case the work should be done according to a seating chart supplied by the conductor. Minor adjustments in the seating plan may, of course, be made in the rehearsal proper. It should not be necessary to state that the members of the organization should be assigned definite locations subject to change only by the conductor. The day of the "sit-where-you-please" type of musical organization is happily past in most schools. Seating assignments should be made according to a definite plan and for specific educational purposes which will be explained in detail in a later chapter.

The problem of music distribution has been met successfully by the "self-serve" storage cabinet which is now in fairly common use. This system is so far superior to any other plan that conductors who have not given it a trial would do well to investigate its time-saving possibilities without further delay. The cabinet itself is simply a single or double tier of shelves, perferably with doors which may be locked or at least closed for the protection of the music. The shelves are labelled and numbered by sections to correspond to the music folders. The folders are prepared by the conductor or his helpers and are placed on the proper shelves in advance of the first rehearsal. As soon as seating assignments have been made, instructions covering the use and care of the music are given. From then on the system practically operates itself. At the beginning of the rehearsal one player at each desk takes the music folder from the cabinet and at the end of the period it is returned to the proper shelf. If a player wishes to check out the folder for individual practice, he merely signs and dates a large card which remains on the cabinet shelf at all times. Whenever a particular folder is not in the cabinet, the signed card will indicate which player has the music and when it was taken out. Under this system, or in fact under any other system, the player must agree to return all music to every rehearsal regardless of any expense or inconvenience which may be involved.

The checking of attendance is another chore which should, if possible, be delegated to an assistant or to one or more of the student officers of the organization. The easiest method is to make the check by sections, and some teachers prefer to use a seating chart for this purpose. In this connection, the placing in advance of the exact number of chairs required proves extremely helpful. A vacant chair means an absent member and it becomes a relatively easy matter to discover which player is not in attendance. Late arrivals should also be checked very carefully as they may be a greater handicap to the organization than those who remain away entirely. Whether the attendance checking is done by the conductor or by some other person, the record must be accurate in every detail in order that any later controversy on the matter may be settled on the basis of fact rather than guesswork. Regular attendance is vital to the success of any musical organization because the entire group suffers from the absence of a single member. A missed rehearsal can never be "made up."

One of the most widely circulated of the early texts on the organization of instrumental music groups stated that the so-called "warm up" period should properly be conducted in *perfect silence*. The writer most emphatically disagrees with this point of view, and a few of the most obvious reasons are stated here in support of this opinion. While it is theoretically possible to warm a horn or a woodwind instrument in silence, or at least without producing an audible musical tone, this is certainly not the most effective method, and it contributes absolutely nothing to the "warm up" of the players' lips. (The term "warm up" is used for want of a better one and because it is universally employed and understood by both amateur and professional players.) No one has yet discovered a satisfactory method of "warming up" a stringed instrument and its player without actual playing of the instrument. The player's arms, hands, and fingers must be adjusted to the instrument in preparation for the exacting demands of the rehearsal, and in the same way the player of every other instrument must recapture the "feel" of his instrument after having been engaged in other types of activities. From a purely physical standpoint this period of adjustment is most essential, but even more important is the fact that by this means a correct mental attitude toward the rehearsal is established.

The warm up period, if properly conducted, may easily become the most important single factor in the development of individual technical skill because it tends to stimulate a purposeful and an analytical attitude toward those problems in the music which have baffled the player in previous rehearsals. An opportunity is provided for the two players at a desk to compare notes and there may even be an element of rivalry in this pre-rehearsal drill on technical detail. This is the one period during which a strong player may be of real help to his weaker partner, and this, incidentally, is an important reason for distributing the strength and the weakness within the organization as widely as possible.

It must be recognized that there are certain dangers inherent in the warm up period, and the conductor of the group would do well to observe the entire procedure with a watchful eye. In fact, so far as his responsibility goes in these matters, the rehearsal starts the minute the first student enters the room, and he should not permit other considerations to distract him from the task of general oversight of the students' activities. For this reason the conductor should urge and insist that all special problems be brought to him at some time other than at the start of the rehearsal. Many students invent problems, partly in order to attract attention, perhaps as an excuse for talking to the teacher, or possibly just because this is a habit of adolescence. Whatever the reason or necessity, the practice should be discouraged because it diverts the attention of the conductor from the group to the individual and makes it impossible for him to properly supervise and direct the organization of the rehearsal. Furthermore, this barrage of special problems during a period of natural and justifiable confusion is apt to leave the conductor in no mood to do his best work in the rehearsal to follow. Only the most poised and self-contained individual could absorb this type of punishment and still be in a proper mental and emotional state to face his group with a smiling face, an inspiring philosophy, and unsounded depths of factual and technical knowledge. To control the situation is most difficult, but surprisingly good results can be achieved by means of two simple devices: the first, by insisting that all problems and questions except those which might be characterized as real emergencies be presented after the rehearsal or after school hours, and the second, by emphasizing repeatedly to the students the importance to them of learning to solve their own problems. This latter measure is certainly in line with the broader concept of the music teacher's social responsibility — the idea that he is not employed solely to teach music but to teach *living* through music — and if he can inculcate in his students some measure of independence in meeting complex or troublesome situations, he will have served well indeed.

Younger students sometimes forget that there is a difference between the rehearsal room and the playground. Wrestling and scuffling endanger valuable equipment and disturb the atmosphere of the rehearsal. The habit of experimentation on different instruments should likewise be discouraged. Tests of endurance in the playing of high and loud tones on the wind instruments should be dealt with in the most effective manner and the one best designed to insure a permanent cure. Students should be encouraged to go to their proper places, with instruments and music, as soon as possible after entering the rehearsal room and then to concentrate upon tuning and drill on the music until the conductor calls the rehearsal to order. The laggards will have to be prodded into line with this program, but eventually they will grasp the general idea that the rehearsal is not the proper place for visiting, loafing, or any other activity not directly related to the business of producing music. In passing, it is advised that the players be urged to leave all instrument cases, school books, and other personal impedimenta in another part of the hall when they take their places in the rehearsal "set-up" proper. Finally, the conductor should be warned that no school official or academic teacher will ever believe that the warm up period is anything but a waste of time, an evidence of poor discipline, and a breeding ground for all those abhorrent qualities which the music program has been accused of injecting into an otherwise orderly institution of learning. Only a musician can appreciate the real beauty of the conglomerate sound which peals forth as the orchestra or band rehearsal gets under way.

Near the beginning of each new semester and as often as is necessary thereafter a general inspection of instruments is in order. While this might be done more effectively at another time, there is a certain psychological advantage in doing it in the general rehearsal,

46270

and it need not require a great amount of time if the matter is well organized. To be wholly effective a written record of the findings should be made by a student secretary appointed for the purpose. Needed repairs or adjustments and lack of required supplementary equipment such as mutes for strings and brass instruments, and extra reeds for the woodwinds should stand on the record against the individual until the specific items are checked off in person with the conductor. To conduct this inspection in the general rehearsal emphasizes the importance of having the instruments in the best possible condition, and by this method the conductor is sure to reach all members of the group. No more embarrassing situation is likely to present itself than the discovery near the end of the school year that cornet tuning slides have become immovable through corrosion, that several of the stringed instruments are loose in the joints, or that a leading clarinet player has been using for some weeks an instrument which is functioning only with the aid of pieces of string, rubber bands, toothpicks, and chewing-gum.

A controversy of long standing is that concerning the relative merits of beginning the rehearsal with a march or some other loud and lively number, with a slow-moving number of the choral type, with individual and unison tuning, or with some form of chord tuning. All of these methods are employed by band and orchestra conductors with varying degrees of success. Some follow a fixed pattern of procedure for all rehearsals while others adapt the approach to the particular situation in terms of the results which they wish to obtain immediately. The conductor, if he is to be successful, must be a good judge of human nature and extremely sensitive to the reactions of individuals and groups to various conditions and circumstances. The manner in which he opens the rehearsal will prove an exacting test of his capacity as an analyst of temper and temperament. If, for example, he should undertake a decidedly careful and detailed general check of tuning at the outset of a typical "blue Monday" rehearsal, or if he should devote a considerable amount of time to chord tuning and the playing of chorales immediately following an all-school football assembly, he would be inviting disaster. Both of these situations would suggest opening with the playing of some lively tune until, in the first instance, the group could be revived from its week-end lethargy and, in the second instance, could be brought gradually under some semblance of control. These conditions will be the exception, not the rule, and there will be a great many rehearsals in which the musical morale is extremely high and the students prepared to accept with enthusiasm the most meticulous analyses and the most painstaking drill. Occasionally it may even be possible to open the rehearsal with an analysis of one of the compositions, but the general rule should be to "talk little and play much," especially at the beginning of the rehearsal.

In order to insure at least an acceptable pitch agreement among the various instruments at the start, many conductors have adopted one or two basic tuning chords for their organizations, and these chords may even be used for the final check before an audience with a fair degree of satisfaction. For the orchestra, one good chord is the D minor triad, since it includes the two strings which are common to all stringed instruments plus the concert F, a natural tuning note for the French horn. This chord also permits the testing of the cornet open G, the second valve B and the first and second valve E, and with it the clarinets can test their G in three octaves, utilizing three different tube lengths. Another chord is the dominant seventh chord: A, C sharp, E, and G. This chord includes even a greater variety of open-string tones. For the band, the E-flat and B-flat major triads are reasonably easy to play in tune, but a more efficient test would be one including such naturally out-of-tune notes as the major triad on C, concert pitch. This chord demands the use of the difficult third valve (in combination) for all of the brass instruments in B-flat, E-flat and F, but it could be given a bit more stability by adding the minor seventh, B-flat. A brief sounding of some such basic chord at the opening of the rehearsal, and the group is ready to proceed with the study of new material for a time, even though a more exhaustive test of tuning might be undertaken later in the rehearsal.

A question which is almost certain to arise is one bearing upon the amount of rehearsal time to be devoted to the various phases of training. Needless to say, any answer that might be given is in the nature of a compromise since there is never enough time in which to accomplish all of the things one has in prospect. The emphasis will be governed by the immediate demands in the way of public appearances which the organization faces, the amount of technical training necessary to bring the group up to an acceptable level of performing ability, the need of a broader acquaintanceship with orchestra or band literature, or other like considerations which may vary from week to week. Certainly it would be unwise, in a rehearsal of ordinary length, to attempt too many different types of activity, as this practice could only lead to confusion and a fragmentary development of ideas and techniques. Following are a few of the categories into which the rehearsal time might be divided: 1. chord tuning; 2. individual or unison tuning; 3. unison scales or exercises for rhythm, bowing, or articulation; 4. review playing of material already learned; 5. sight-reading of new material of an easier grade (such numbers should be played without pauses for corrections); 6. combined reading, analysis, and drill on new material of the highest grade of difficulty consistent with the ability of the group; 7. ensemble "stunts" such as transposition, playing tunes by ear, practice in counting aloud, and the singing of instrumental parts.

Of these the basic procedures are, of course, tuning, study of new material, and sight-reading. Tuning is necessary in order to insure satisfactory results in the general playing, although many conductors regard even this as a problem which will find its own solution in subsequent drill by sections and the full ensemble. This is easily possible if constant emphasis is placed upon accuracy in intonation and if every sustained chord, every duet passage, every solo and accompaniment combination is utilized as a means of stressing careful listening and pitch adjustment. One conductor stated the problem rather well when he asked, "Why waste time tuning those instruments which are already in tune? Tune those which are out of tune if and when the faulty intonation is discovered." This method is quite satisfactory when employed with older or more advanced groups, but elementary orchestras and bands usually require a general preliminary check of tuning and the practice is recommended for all organizations, at least to the extent of sounding a few basic chords.

The study of new material is the principal justification of an organization's existence and hence a very large part of each rehearsal should normally be devoted to this type of activity. In fact, many successful conductors start their rehearsals with the reading-drill-analysis routine and carry it through to the end with only an occasional "summing up" through the performance of a complete overture, symphonic movement, or suite. This method depends for its success entirely upon the conductor's skill in keeping the rehearsal moving toward a definite objective and especially upon his ability to hold the interest of all sections by frequent shifts of attention from one to another, interwoven with the performance of complete passages by the full ensemble. Any failure to include individuals or sections in this study and drill process will cause dissatisfaction and will lead to criticism which is amply justified. The student thrives on the positive assurance that he is achieving something of solid value, and this sense of growth is the inescapable product of the analytical system of study. The use of this method may be justified against any possible objection or criticism by the fact that it is the only one by which the technical and musical deficiencies of individual students may be met. This approach helps the entire ensemble to appreciate the fact that the quality of the finished product is determined by the material and workmanship which go into its several parts.

Many school orchestras and bands have failed to achieve maximum growth as a result of neglect in the field of sight-reading. This widespread failure can be explained but not justified. A few of the deterrent factors are: limited music libraries, inefficient handling of the music, and pressure of contest and concert performances; but ordinary neglect is probably the most common cause of the failure to give instrumentalists the same degree of skill in reading music that they usually possess in reading the printed word. True, there is a physical response required in the reading of music which is not present in the reading of prose or poetry, but this will become more and more habitual if the student's interest in music is increased through more extensive reading. Music should be read and played for the interest and enjoyment which this reading gives to the player. If students were first required to practice reading stories before they could enjoy them, there would be much less interest than there is in reading.

The importance of sight-reading in instrumental music cannot be too strongly emphasized but, on the other hand, a word of caution against placing this activity ahead of other demands might be in order. A balanced program will be found best in the end, and the teacher who places too great an emphasis upon any one phase of instrumental training will erect obstacles in the path of his own progress and that of his students. No fixed rules can be stated for the division of rehearsal time or even for the manner in which the rehearsal is to be conducted, because no two situations will be identical in all respects. Procedures must always be determined by the nature of the group, its objectives, and its obligations. A new organization, or one which is being largely rebuilt, will require more time for instruction and drill than a more mature group which may be called upon for frequent public performances. The more advanced organization will be able to devote a major part of its rehearsal time to reading and the mastery of repertory. Should the conductor misjudge the status and the capacity of his organization and adopt an unsound rehearsal procedure, the group will gradually deteriorate. He must know with reasonable certainty not only the point of departure and the goal, but also the route to be traversed. Whether the start be made at the bottom of the trail or at an intermediate point is of little real importance; the essential thing is that both teacher and student keep striving toward the goal of maximum achievement. For the student this goal is the limit of his ability to learn, and for the teacher it is the limit of his ability to teach. In traversing the upward path both will have to use imagination, resourcefulness, skill, energy, and perseverance; but along with these qualities it is to be hoped that there will be a place for understanding, sympathy, friendliness, and good humor, with a small measure of sternness where indicated. No musical result is worth gaining at the cost of meanness, scolding, petulance, and sarcasm on the part of the teacher, and fear, embarrassment, and loss of confidence on the part of the student. Music, to have any value, must be enjoyed, and so must the process of acquiring musical knowledge and skill. May every rehearsal of a school musical organization be dedicated to the fuller enjoyment of life through music!

CHAPTER V
Problems of Personnel

Music, more than any of the arts except the drama, is a personal art. In its written form music is a product of the mental, emotional, and spiritual reactions of one individual, and in performance it is subject to modification at the hands of still other persons. Ensemble music reflects not only the personality of the conductor but, in many subtle ways, the personality of the players as well; and it is for this reason that so much attention must be given to the study of attitudes and reactions in all types of music ensembles. Upon the individual player's will to perform depends the entire success of the group.

The conductor's first and most important objective must be to preserve whatever natural enthusiasm for musical performance his students may possess and to develop a favorable response by artificial means where the attitude is negative or openly hostile. The attainment of this two-fold objective will depend in part upon the conductor's own attitude, but in addition he will find it advisable to follow certain rather narrowly prescribed rules in dealing with his student personnel. These rules do not differ widely from those generally applicable to any teaching situation except in the fact that an ensemble rehearsal offers greater latitude in all matters than does the classroom recitation.

It is usually safe to assume that a student joins the band or the orchestra because he enjoys playing his instrument and wishes to avail himself of the opportunity for advancement which membership in the group offers. This free choice on the part of the student represents an advantage not always enjoyed by teachers of "required" academic subjects. The preservation of this advantage would not seem to impose undue hardships upon the instrumental teacher, but in too many cases the student loses his enthusiasm and then his interest in the rehearsals. Eventually he reaches the stage of heroic boredom which is but a prelude to permanent desertion from the ranks of the amateur musician.

How best to preserve the student's original desire for this type of activity is a subject worthy of the most careful consideration if for no other reason than to avoid the waste of time, money, and effort involved in these unsuccessful artistic ventures. Every such failure leaves a more or less permanent scar upon the self-confidence of the student, and if repeated in other fields, might be a factor in the development of a "failure complex." It is certainly not to be expected that every student who is persuaded by his parents to take up the study of music will succeed in earning a place for himself in the school orchestra or band; but, provided reasonable fitness is established in advance, the number of complete failures should not be large.

Many clever devices have been invented for the purpose of increasing and holding the membership of school instrumental organizations. These range from the so-called "point" systems, with their elaborate awards and honors, to participation in contests and festivals involving trips to distant cities. Not the least of the glories of membership, especially in the band, is the privilege of wearing an attractive uniform. These stimuli are all perfectly legitimate and have more than justified themselves in providing a focus for both school and community interest in a constructive activity, but it must be recognized that in many cases the very teachers who have instituted these devices for the attraction of students have been guilty of practices which have later tended to repel them. Inadequate musical leadership, slipshod teaching methods, and drill-sergeant tactics in rehearsal are just a few of the more common causes of the withdrawal of students from the music organizations.

No public servant deserves more credit than the music teacher who has been able to attract and hold students, year after year, entirely through the force of his personality, the integrity of his teaching, and the depth of his musicianship without recourse to any of the embellishments commonly employed by the musical charlatan to mask his artistic poverty. Music — great art that it is — should be permitted to speak for itself. Remove the chief obstacles in the form of administrative red tape, provide suitable quarters and adequate library and equipment, employ a teacher who is first a considerate human being and after that a musician, and the instrumental program will serve the purpose intended. The organizations may not be the largest or the flashiest in the area, but the musical product will probably be better for all that, and the students will have something besides medals to take home with them.

The personal and musical qualifications of the teacher and the relationship between teacher and students have been stressed at length because it is felt that these factors are of the utmost importance in the building of an organization. Consider, for example, the somewhat routine matter of seating assignments in terms of the personality questions involved.

Under an older and widely accepted method of determining the order in which the players should be seated, a system of playing trials or tests was employed. Under the operation of this method the strongest players were presumably determined and they were placed according to a prearranged plan in certain key positions. To a mechanically minded individual this system presents distinct advantages; but to one who places personal values above material values, or who sees the possibility of material gain through the development of personality, this plan has definite shortcomings. In the one instance, a competitive activity based largely upon technical skill is used to determine the seating order; whereas in the other, musicianship, technical ability, personality, temperament, experience, and innumerable other factors are taken into account. In the first case the decision is made by the students; in the other it is made by the teacher who is presumed to have special and essentially pedagogical reasons for his decisions in the matter. For example, the wise teacher will place a player who is strong in rhythm at the same desk with one who is weak in rhythm. He will pair a violinist whose bowing is good but whose intonation is weak with one whose bowing needs to be developed but who has a keen sense of pitch and an accurate left-hand technique. He may temporarily place a timid but competent player in a position of responsibility as a means of developing that player's self-assurance, and conversely he may "deflate" another player by requiring him to play in a secondary position for a time. He has even been known to assign a particular boy a seat beside a particular girl as a means of increasing the interest of both in the orchestra! Such are the strange devices of the conductor who knows his players and human nature and is prepared to use this knowledge for the advancement of the cause of music and his own organization.

The social and scholastic standings of orchestras and bands vary widely in different institutions. In some schools these organizations include in their membership an unduly large proportion of academic outcasts — those students who represent the fringe of educational respectability. For some reason not always easy to discover, problem cases frequently find their way into the instrumental music organizations. Students with poor scholastic records, adjustment difficulties, and doubtful moral fiber seem to gravitate toward all of the so-called and misnamed extra-curricular activities. After observing this process of the infiltration of the undesirables for a time, one is led to suspect the existence of an undercover plot to provide these students with the shell of an education at the expense of the music, athletic, and manual arts departments. If this is proved to be the case, the villain in the plot is probably the school principal; but he is aided and abetted by those faculty members who reason that if a boy cannot solve problems in algebra, he should at least be able to play a drum, a trombone, or even a violin.

Fortunately such cases of administrative and staff ignorance and discrimination are rare, but it is well for the music teacher to be aware of the fact that, in isolated cases, such reasoning may result in his having to accept more than his share of the school's problem cases. For his own protection and the protection of his organization he may find it necessary or desirable to follow a definite procedure designed to establish and maintain the prestige of the group.

At first glance it might seem best to include in the instrumental organizations as many as possible of those students who are not engaged in other special activities, on the theory that these students will have more time for practice and for the other outside activities of the orchestra or band. This view is a mistaken one as most successful music directors can testify. There is an old adage to the effect that if you have a job to do, ask the busiest man you know to do it. The reasoning back of this is that a busy man is busy because he is capable — because he has learned to do things quickly and efficiently. The man who is not busy may lack the wit, the skill, or the personality to undertake many and varied tasks. The same rule applies to a school situation. The leaders in the student body possess ability, enthusiasm, brains, and all of the other qualities which make for success. They will usually be able to contribute more to the musical organization, even with less training and less practice, than many of the players who devote their entire time and attention to musical pursuits. Further, the acquisition of one school leader as a member of the orchestra or the band will attract others and will stimulate younger students to take up the study of instruments. This policy, if followed to its logical conclusion, should increase the standing and the popularity of the instrumental groups and should attract into the membership of these organizations students who possess those personal and intellectual qualities which are vital to the performance of, and the proper interpretation of, good music. An article which is constructed of poor material will ever remain the same. Quality cannot be superimposed upon a shoddy basic substance. No orchestra or band can execute with understanding and technical skill or interpret with imagination and feeling unless the capacity for these achievements is inherent in the personality of the players themselves. The acceptance of this fact would seem to justify a deliberate effort on the part of both conductor and school administrator to interest the most talented students in the performance of instrumental music while at the same time not excluding from the benefits of this work any less gifted student who is sufficiently interested to contribute to the limit of his capacity.

Most music teachers have been faced, at one time or another, with problems of discipline. Some regard these unhappy episodes with calm stoicism and do not allow them to disturb an otherwise peaceful existence. Others, of a different temperament, suffer acutely as a result of any misunderstanding or friction with students. The technique of handling such cases varies with the disposition, poise, self-control, and bulk of the particular teacher. Sometimes the outcome is quite satisfactory; frequently it proves professionally disastrous to the teacher.

One of the very best methods of handling discipline problems is to avoid them entirely, an achievement which is sometimes extremely difficult but seldom impossible. A number of suggestions bearing upon teacher attitudes and organizational techniques which should be of some help to the instrumental music teacher are contained in this and earlier chapters. These hints are somewhat general in character and should perhaps be supplemented by some more specific instances of disciplinary technique.

A good first rule is to have a student organization with elected officers who will have specific duties to perform in connection with the rehearsals. Make friends with as many of the students as possible, and especially with those you are not sure can be counted upon.

Seek out the possible trouble-makers and put yourself under some small moral obligation to them by asking them to do something *for you*. If any sort of difficulty arises in rehearsal be sure to discuss the matter in private with the student concerned. Never reprimand a student before others. This is the good old oriental philosophy of "face saving." Always try to be encouraging and helpful in making corrections. Instead of criticizing a student, show him the proper approach to his problem and make him feel that most of what he has done is quite all right, that only certain details require improvement. Be as pleasant as possible at all times. Seek out special tasks at which certain members of the group excel and thus tie them to the organization through their own special interests. If, in your manner, you can show that you enjoy the company of the students, your attitude will probably be reflected in theirs.

This whole matter of personal relationships and attitudes may be regarded by some as of considerably less importance than its treatment here would seem to indicate. There is ample room for honest differences of opinion on this and other points, but one must always be extremely careful in evaluating the results of one or the other method of handling a particular situation. The teacher who believes in hard-boiled efficiency in the rehearsal at the cost of pleasant human relationships will usually find that the performance has lost much of the warmth, fervor, freshness, and vitality that might otherwise have characterized it. Students who have been driven, threatened, and scolded will play with a degree of muscular, mental, and emotional tenseness not usually present in the work of those organizations which have been encouraged to do their best by an inspired and an inspiring leader.

An almost perfect illustration of this difference in group reaction was that observed some years ago in one of the regional music contests. In this particular event the stage curtain was dropped between performances but the audience could hear distinctly all that transpired backstage as each of the orchestras took its place. The entry of one group was characterized by general confusion and a good deal of loud talking, in which the directions and commands of the conductor predominated. When the curtain was raised the general order and appearance of the orchestra was disappointing and its performance left still more to be desired. In contrast to this exhibition of poor training, the following orchestra took its place on the

stage so quickly and so quietly that the audience was made aware
of its presence only by a general hearty laugh which issued from
behind the stage curtain. This spontaneous outburst subsided in-
stantly, the curtain was raised, and there on the stage was one of the
finest-appearing school orchestras ever to be assembled. The arrangement was perfect, the dress was dignified and uniform, the
posture was easy and correct throughout, and the group played like
angels! The performance was characterized by excellent intonation,
entirely adequate technical skill, and a sweep and breadth of style
that would have done credit to a professional group. The program
which this group played included standard symphonic material!

Now it is just possible that there exists not even a remote connection between the evidence of poor spirit and poor discipline, and
the unsatisfactory musical results produced by the first organization;
and it is also possible that the wholesome attitude and the efficiency
of the second group were in no way related to its performance, but
the suggestion is there for those who may wish to consider the matter in its relation to educational practice and philosophy.

Whatever views one may hold with reference to contests as an
aid to the advancement of music education, it will be recognized
that they have constituted a most interesting laboratory for the
study of human reactions. The instance cited above is but one of
many which suggest that one of the chief values of music as a
medium of education is that, through music more than through
most other subject matter, the teacher can quickly and effectively
bring his influence to bear upon the student. This presupposes, of
course, that he be a teacher and not merely a drill-master, a baton-
wielder, or a musical aesthete.

The music contests expanded and intensified the potentialities of
music as a medium of general and cultural education; but, organized
primarily for the purpose of increasing interest in group participation, they soon grew into unwieldy carnivals in which purely musical considerations played a poor second to problems of transporta-
tion, housing, and feeding. In the later years of the regional-national
contests it was no uncommon occurrence for the largest and finest
orchestras and bands to perform with practically no audience present to hear their splendid work. A few friends and parents would
remain for the performance of the group in which they were particularly interested, and shortly their places would be taken by the

supporters of the next organization to appear. And still, even in the absence of any continuous attendance upon a particular contest event, how certain these adherents usually were of the superiority of their own organizations! This was only one of the interesting phenomena connected with the music contest.

The question of the objectives which teachers and students had in mind as they prepared for the contests presents a study which is not unrelated to the general subject of this chapter. Were those objectives to increase the students' love of music, their technical skill, their appreciation of the artistic, were they to improve the professional standing of the teacher, were they to advertise the community, or were they to provide trips and recreation for large numbers of high school students? In the minds of different persons any one of these several objectives may have assumed importance, and they were probably all present in the thinking of the public which supported the contest movement so liberally for so many years. Fortunately, perhaps, for the cause of honest music education, the war brought a temporary end to music contests on the grand scale and it is to be hoped that they will not be resumed until such time as music educators have an opportunity to reexamine and reevaluate the fundamental objectives in this field.

Always a firm supporter of the contest as an educational device, as a means of enlisting public support, and as a guarantee of student interest, the writer first began to question its benefits when he became aware of the intensive drill methods which were employed by many teachers in their desire to have their groups win. This usually meant the neglect of real teaching in the broader sense and an undue emphasis upon the attainment of technical proficiency at the expense of musical understanding, practice in sight-reading, and acquaintanceship with a widely representative repertory.

The narrow objective is well illustrated by the case of the orchestra director who, as his group was about to leave the tuning room for the contest stage, belabored the students with a "pep talk" which sent them into the event in a state of nervous tension which could not fail to make any worthwhile performance impossible. In this case the results were quite pitiful and the reaction of the students following the event did no credit either to the conductor or to his method of approach. Such instances have been sufficiently common to cause the observer to wonder what good over-all cause is served by the pressure philosophy. Surely some means can be found of preserving the benefits of widespread participation in musical performance without subjecting students to the curse of nervous fatigue, discouragement, and disillusionment.

It must be remembered that teachers and students alike react differently to any given situation. Consider the case of the orchestra director who has taught so substantially that the performance of the contest numbers is a natural outgrowth of a systematic development of both skills and understanding. Even under such circumstances some special emphasis on the contest pieces is required, but the work should be done with calm deliberation and with a sane and balanced outlook on the part of both teacher and students. With such an approach the final word of the teacher before the contest need only be to call the players' attention to the benefits they have derived from the study of the material, to urge that they profit from hearing the performances of other groups, and to suggest that they make their own performance as interesting as possible to the listeners. To establish such a mood and to studiously omit any mention of the outcome of the contest, will usually produce far more satisfactory results than to stress the competitive element. Actually, the correct attitude must be built up over a long period of time before the contest takes place. Where this is done, the event itself is only an episode along the road to musical development.

This matter of the proper psychological approach to a contest performance is treated here at some length because of the importance of these principles in all forms of public appearance. Each time that a group performs in concert the conductor must study anew the mental attitudes of his players and build toward the specific event. No two situations will call for exactly the same procedure. If the numbers to be played have not been too well prepared the director will find it advisable to employ every known device for improving the technical grasp, but he will also strive to strengthen the players' confidence and assurance. If old material is being performed there may be a tendency toward laxity on the part of the players, in which case the conductor should try to read into the interpretation of the work some new values, perhaps by calling for a more elastic pulsation, a lighter style, or a broader resonance in the playing of harmonic passages—anything, in fact, that will inject a new interest into the work of preparation. There are many ways of altering the emphasis to give a well-known composition a fresh appeal to the players and thus to insure a better performance.

Most important of all, the conductor must induce in his players an attitude toward the concert which is alert and positive — the feeling that the particular concert is something toward which they should look with pleasurable anticipation. If a group can go onto the concert stage with the feeling that the hard work has been done and that they are now prepared to enjoy themselves and to give pleasure to others, the performance will invariably be successful. The conductor who deals with amateurs must do his best at all times to eliminate careless execution and slovenly reading habits in rehearsals; but when the time for the concert arrives, his attitude must be: What of a few minor technical slips among friends, especially if the spirit is right and the performance generally sincere and honest? Strangely enough, this mental approach will usually guarantee the best possible performance. No student will take advantage of such a tolerant attitude on the part of the teacher, especially before his friends and in public performance. He will, if he has a normal mentality, try all the harder to do a good piece of work to show the conductor that such excusable technical slips can be avoided.

Opportunities for the application of similar psychological principles in rehearsals and concerts, and in the teacher's dealings with individual students, are practically unlimited. Their employment in the prevention and solution of problems should be the subject of constant study on the part of the teacher. It might almost be said that the proper psychological approach, meaning simply the capacity to understand the reactions of individuals and groups to particular situations, will be the final determining factor in the success of the teacher. Certainly it plays a very large part in an art field in which the interest and enthusiasm of the individual plays so important a part in the attainment of the desired objectives.

CHAPTER VI

Choice of Musical Materials

The really important growth in the number and quality of school orchestras and bands has taken place in the last quarter century. During this period the educational status of the instrumental musical organizations has changed so greatly as to leave little room for even the most superficial comparison.

In 1917, the year of this country's entry into the first World War, the ordinary school band was a haphazard, nondescript group of players usually organized by the students themselves chiefly as a "pep band" to enliven athletic rallies and games. These bands seldom had uniforms, their instruments were privately owned and usually represented an assortment of pitches ranging from the high pitch of an earlier day to the low pitch which is now fairly standard, they had only such music as might have been borrowed for their immediate needs, there were no regular rehearsals, and these bands seldom enjoyed the advantage of professional leadership. There were a few exceptions to this general rule, but in practically no instance was the band regarded as an integral part of the educational program.

During this period the school orchestras were no further advanced than the bands. If and when they existed it was on an exceedingly temporary basis, usually in support of an amateur stage production of some sort. These were the days of the old "theater orchestra," and it was not uncommon for the schools to follow the example of the professionals by organizing small "pit orchestras" for class plays and even, under more ambitious leadership, to provide accompaniments for operas or cantatas. As an indication of the state of the instrumental music program in the not-too-distant past it might be mentioned that the author of this text was one of the student-organizers of the first orchestra to continue as a permanent organization in a high school which had an enrollment of almost two thousand students. To further indicate the rapidity of the growth in this field, not only in that community but over the country at large, there existed in this same school some fifteen years later, five large instrumental organizations supported by innumerable junior high school and grade school orchestras, bands, and instrumental classes of various kinds.

As has been stated, this astounding growth was attributed by some to the impetus supplied by the army bands during the period of World War I. Certainly the availability of large numbers of men trained in army bands either as conductors or as players must have been a contributing factor, but back of it all there was a changing concept of the function of public education. In the years that followed up to the start of World War II there was no material change in this trend, at least in its effect upon the general music program.

The suddenness with which this wave of interest in instrumental music swept through the schools of the country found the teachers of music and the publishers of educational materials totally unprepared. Instrumental methods and special editions of school orchestra and band music of the type now in use were non-existent. Conductors and teachers were forced to depend upon the so-called "studio methods" as instructional material and upon folios and single numbers designed for use by cafe and theater orchestras as ensemble training material and, in fact, for program purposes. The school bands followed the pattern and used the literature of the professional bands of the day, which were for the most part out-of-door concert organizations in which the brass and percussion instruments predominated. Quantities of this old music may still be found in school band libraries and occasionally it serves a useful purpose in spite of its deficiencies in instrumentation and arrangement.

As a direct result of the dearth of really suitable and worthy music and the difficulty of obtaining original editions, the school groups were compelled to make the best of a difficult situation. The most widely used set of beginning methods for single instruments required editing to keep the young students within reasonable range limits; this material advanced far too rapidly, and much essential matter had been omitted entirely. The standard in orchestra literature was a certain series of folios which contained the cheapest sort of musical material. The string parts of these books could be bowed only by skilled professional players, so badly organized were they in the matter of proper sequence of down- and up-bows. This series was later arranged for school bands, and in order to keep the parts within a suitable range for the wind instruments the melodies were frequently altered midway by an octave shift downward or upward as might be required!

Another popular folio, so arranged as to be playable by either orchestra or band, contained distorted simplifications of operatic arias and other pieces, in addition to several original numbers by the publisher! These arrangements were models of flexibility. They could be used by almost any combination of instruments from two violins and a full complement of brass, to one cornet, three clarinets, and twenty violins. Still a third contribution to school instrumental literature was one based upon the theory that no violinist liked to play second violin, so why have second violin parts? All violin parts were, therefore, written as melodic voices. After using this material for one year the conductor usually discovered that none of his violinists were able to play the "after-beat" parts occasionally found in standard arrangements. No viola part was provided with this folio, but it could be played by a band by using the wind books of the set and eliminating the strings! Such was the material with which the earlier conductors were forced to contend.

Happily, this condition of affairs has changed within recent years, and the credit for the improvement should go to many persons and organizations. Individual teachers who pointed the way to better things musically by making use of really fine standard music in original editions have perhaps exerted the greatest influence. Teacher-training institutions have given their students a somewhat better musical background and have sent them into the teaching field with a more discriminating taste and understanding. More *musicians* are now teaching music than was formerly the case. The decline in the professional playing field, occasioned by the introduction of the sound-on-film moving pictures, forced a great many competent musicians to seek livelihoods and careers in school music. The radio has probably raised the general level of music appreciation, although it takes a patient and persistent dial-twirler to separate the musical wheat from the chaff of jazz, crooning, and light "pieces." The National High School Orchestra, organized by Joseph E. Maddy and presented before the National Education Association on several occasions, and other large orchestras and bands which have appeared before sectional and national meetings of the Music Educators National Conference have been both a cause and a result of the widespread interest in instrumental music in the schools. The Music Educators National Conference itself has for almost forty years been an influence for growth in this and other fields. The so-called instrumental "clinics," patterned after the one held for many years at the University of Illinois under the stimulating leadership of A. A. Harding, have been important factors. Summer music camps, contests, and festivals have all played their separate parts in this artistic revolution.

The lack of suitable musical material in the early days of the movement was due largely to the fact that previously there had been no demand for anything better. The musical groups that had existed before that time were mere accessories to some other form of activity. But with the growth and expansion of the entire program, bands and orchestras became musical entities, supported and maintained in their own right as concert organizations. This, in turn, provided a constant and permanent market for new publications, better instruments, and all sorts and descriptions of supplementary equipment. The music trades responded to this growing demand in many different ways, depending upon the musical, ethical, and business instincts of the leaders.

Some firms saw in the movement an opportunity to profit enormously through a quick turnover of music and goods. These were the establishments which provided us with the horns that fell apart during the first year, the clarinets which were permanently out of tune, and music which would sell on sight but which contributed little to growth in musicianship. These same firms flooded the market for a time with melody saxophones, on the strength of national advertising which asserted that they could be learned practically overnight. Other, and more ethical, establishments looked further into the future and saw a much more substantial market for better instruments and better music in the days ahead, and these firms usually consulted with the leading music educators in the formulation of their policies. Both types of publishers, manufacturers, and dealers were, admittedly, in business for the same purpose – to make money – but one group helped the cause of music education, whereas the other group only placed obstacles in the path of progress. In recent years the music trades have shown an increasing desire and capacity to work with the music educators in the advancement of a common cause.

The problem of selecting material for use by the school band and orchestra leads inevitably to a consideration of the question of the functions and purposes of these organizations. Are they maintained primarily to serve the school and community in connection with athletic events, civic celebrations, concerts, and the like; or do they exist chiefly as media for education through the development of special skills and the cultivation of artistic attitudes? The obvious answer is that under the best conditions of leadership and public support school bands and orchestras should serve both of these desirable ends. To ignore the service function would result in loss of public interest in the organizations and would deprive the students of a valuable incentive for continued membership, while to slight the educational feature would remove the last argument for the inclusion of instrumental music in the school curriculum at public expense.

The extent to which an organization serves both of these primary functions — service and education — will be reflected in the catalogue of its library. If the band library, for example, contains little else but street marches, popular tunes, novelty numbers, and light overtures it is a fair indication that the director has lost sight of his obligation to develop players in the field of musicianship. If, on the other hand, the library includes only concert material it may be assumed that the general service function of the band is being neglected. In either of these extreme cases there is evidence of lack of balance which should be corrected forthwith if the organization hopes to merit the support of its members, the school, and the community.

The music library should include examples of the best available material in each of the various categories. There are good, bad, and indifferent street marches, to be judged upon the basis of melodic content, harmonic interest, construction, dynamic variation, and arrangement. Even some of the best-known marches are unsuited for actual parade use due chiefly to excessive difficulty. For the best results the director will avoid marches employing extreme ranges, awkward melodic skips, after-beats in the trombone parts, and difficult harmonic sequences.

If popular song numbers are included in the library, they should be selected with the greatest of care. Only those, the titles and texts of which are in unquestionable good taste, should even be considered for use by school groups. In this regard it is wise to be con-

servative and safe. Good melodies, and texts based upon decent senti-
ment, characterize the best of the popular tunes; and such material
is most likely to win a lasting place in American folk music. Novelty
tunes should be clever and interesting and they should have something to recommend them other than the mere fact that they are
novelties. Barnyard imitations and rowdy plagarisms of serious
works would seem to have little place on any program sponsored by
an educational institution.

Light concert pieces and overtures can also reflect to a considerable degree the discriminating taste of the director, or they can be
musically inferior and practically worthless either as entertainment
or as education.

The foregoing paragraphs have dealt chiefly with those types of
musical material which are required to satisfy the public service
functions of school bands and orchestras. In addition there should
be in the library a considerable quantity of music which has been
selected primarily for educational purposes. Much of this material
may never be performed publicly, either because the local public is
not likely to appreciate its form and style or because its value as
training material outweighs its merits as program material. Few
amateur groups can perform acceptably a composition in an extremely sustained style, yet such a number might make an invaluable
contribution to the technical and musical development of the individuals in the group. Much of the music used for sight-reading
practice, for example, might be unsuited to public performance, but
this fact should not limit its inclusion in the library or its use in the
rehearsal. Some music, too difficult for program use, is invaluable for
drill purposes. Or perhaps the director will wish to use only portions
of standard works as a means of teaching specific skills. Thus it may
be seen that there are many excellent reasons for including in the
library a good deal of material other than that which is actually
required for public performance. It is in the choice of this material,
especially, that the teacher is urged to exercise the utmost discrimination. This music will constitute the core of his teaching program
and in its selection and use for training purposes he should be guided
solely by his own musical taste. The choice of materials, of course,
will always be made with the technical limitations of his players in
mind.

Faced with the task of determining what should be included in this select category of the best music, many teachers would perhaps experience difficulty in making a wise selection. Certainly no two lists would be identical, but lists compiled by a number of well-trained and discriminating teachers would be likely to include a good many titles in common. The question is one which merits a great deal of careful study.

There are, of course, certain technical rules for the determination of musical quality. The rules of harmony, counterpoint, and form must be respected, or at least any disregard of these rules must be justified by the ultimate musical satisfaction attained through their violation. The rules of proper combination of instruments must be followed unless, again, a very special effect is desired, and this effect must be distinctive and purposeful to justify the means employed. The melodic material must be pleasing, it must serve to arouse some particular emotion, or it must appeal to the intellect of the listener through symmetry or interest of line. It may be subtle but it should not be trite or repetitious. Beauty of phrasing and a smooth inter-locking of melodic material often mark the composition of distinc-tion. In a work of real merit the subject matter is developed and coordinated, and any accompanying figurations are appropriate to the general spirit of the work. The obvious is left unsaid. Suggestion and subtlety stand in place of sordid display. The diverse tastes and preferences of listeners make it difficult, if not impossible, to estab-lish sound bases for evaluating the worth of particular compositions, but some conclusions can usually be reached by applying these ele-mentary tests:

1. Is it interesting melodically, harmonically, or rhythmically?
2. Does it seem to have balance and proportion?
3. Does it have basic unity and cohesion?
4. Are instrumentation and arrangement satisfactory?

The composer who is both a creative artist and a skillful workman will usually produce something of value. The task which the con-ductor must always face is that of eliminating the cheap and the shoddy and of preserving that which grows in beauty and strength with closer acquaintance. The extent to which he succeeds in ful-filling this task may in some measure determine his fitness for mu-sical leadership.

When Diogenes took his lantern in hand and set forth in quest of an honest man, he faced no more difficult task than does the conductor of a school band or orchestra when he searches for material suitable for concert performance. To enumerate just a few of the more obvious specifications, the music must be of sufficiently good quality to meet the standard which he has set for himself and his students, and this standard must pass muster before the local public. The music selected must be playable by the instrumentation which is available. It should not be chosen if it contains essential material in parts for instruments which are either missing entirely or for instruments on which the players are inexperienced. The style and mood of the composition must suit the occasion; and if several numbers are to be presented, they should bear a proper relationship in matters of key, meter, tempo, dynamics, and melodic content. For example, one might easily make the mistake of selecting several numbers in the same basic meter and tempo, with the result that the entire performance would lack audience interest. The length of the numbers is also an important consideration. Some conductors solve this problem by the liberal insertion of "cuts," a practice which is open to serious criticism on the grounds that it destroys and mutilates the musical form as conceived by the composer. In selecting music for contest purposes many conductors have failed to take into consideration the fundamental purpose of a contest performance, which is to demonstrate to the listeners and to the judges all of the things which the orchestra or band can do well. It is not enough to present a contest performance which is limited to the style of playing which the group can do best, as this leaves it up to the judges to guess whether or not the organization can play other styles with equal effectiveness. A contest performance should, therefore, include contrasting technical and musical material for the purpose of proving conclusively that the group possesses skill, musicianship, and artistic versatility. These are but a few of the principal questions involved in the selection of material, and when the limited choice offered by most school music libraries is considered, the problem becomes even more difficult.

In purchasing music for the library it is well to make certain of the quality and content of the music before making final commitments. One method is to hear the music played by another school group and to supplement this hearing by a study of the score and parts. Every teacher has in his library a few choice numbers which have been tested and proved in the light of musical content, suitability, and utility. One of the safest means of building a satisfactory library is to consult others in the profession who have demonstrated their ability as teachers and their discrimination as program builders.

A common misconception is that good music is necessarily difficult music. Nothing could be farther from the truth. What could be easier, both technically and musically, than the old German chorales? They are perfectly adapted to the needs of tone production, intonation, and balance, besides providing substantial melodic and harmonic interest. In the better transcriptions of the easier symphony movements, short pieces, suites, and songs of Bach, Gluck, Rameau, Handel, Haydn, Mozart, Purcell, Chopin, Schumann, Schubert, and Beethoven, we find a practically unlimited supply of the richest sort of material for school orchestras. Much of this great musical wealth is available in arrangements for younger bands.

More advanced orchestras and those having complete instrumentation need not concern themselves with special school orchestra editions but may go directly to the sources of standard symphonic literature. There is no real reason for the use of simplified editions by the largest and best orchestras since, for example, it has been demonstrated that high school trombone players can learn to read the tenor clef and that the horn and trumpet players can learn to transpose from the original parts. This is all a legitimate part of their musical education. For such orchestras, and this includes the better college and university orchestras, the original editions should be used wherever possible, and the greatest care should be exercised in avoiding the mistakes of the "modernized" versions. To insert trombones and tuba where none were included by the composer or to rearrange the woodwind parts as has been done in many of the newer editions not only destroys the original concept of the work but leads to still further tampering with an art work which should be permitted to remain as the composer wrote it.

When we begin to consider the selection of band music, we face a most difficult situation. The history of the development of the band has been wholly unfavorable to the natural growth of a literature comparable to that which we find for the orchestra. The band has always been either an adjunct to the military establishment or an open-air concert unit of doubtful artistic standards. The very conditions under which the bands of the past were called upon to perform were prejudicial to the development of a proper instrumentation or the creation of a literature worthy of the name. True, the band had its own literature, but this was hardly the type of music that could be brought indoors when the band assumed the respectability of a balanced symphonic concert organization. The musical content was unsuited to concert-hall performance, and the instrumentation could hardly have been worse.

As a result of trying to build a new function into an old machine, blunders and mistakes were made, and we are still in the process of trying to reconstruct both the organization and its music. Whereas the orchestra has a fairly standard instrumentation and seating arrangement, the band still faces a chaotic condition in these matters. The literature consists for the most part of transcriptions of orchestral, piano, or organ literature, and the band faces the inevitable difficulty of trying to make these "de-rangements" sound as effective as they do in their original form. This is usually impossible, and as a result many musicians assume a critical attitude toward the band and its music. The harshest critic, if he had first-hand knowledge of the situation, would be the first to admit the difficulty of the band conductor's task.

For the band conductor who has no artistic ideals no special problem is presented. He plays what material is available with little appreciation of its artistic shortcomings and little thought of the means which might be employed to improve the final product. Matters of tonal balance, lack of sostenuto, restricted range, overlapping of mixed voicings, inartistic writing for the percussion instruments, violation of key relationships, simplifications which destroy the original character of well-known passages, and numerous other items which would irritate a more sensitive artist are accepted as matters of course. In fact, it may be said without fear of contradiction that it requires more skill, more resourcefulness, more imagination, and more hard work to achieve artistic results with a band than with an orchestra of the same advancement. Some directors will claim that they can get quicker results with band than with orchestra, but this has no direct bearing upon the point in question. The higher levels of artistic achievement present greater difficulties for the band than for the orchestra because of the lack of tonal flexibility and many other practical considerations which will be appreciated by those conductors who have worked conscientiously with both types of organizations.

Just as the conductor of the band must exert constant watchfulness in matters of tonal clarity, mechanical smoothness, and musical flexibility, so must he guard against the temptation to accept a lower standard in the choice of music. The men who have written for orchestra have been among the world's greatest musicians; few truly great musicians have written for band except experimentally or by special request. Had these composers known the modern symphonic band with its improved balance, its well-constructed instruments, and its generally acceptable tone quality and intonation, there is little question that they would have written some really great music for band. May the composers of the future make amends for the neglect of their confrères of the past! The modern band deserves the best musical literature that can be provided.

Young bands should be given a rich diet of chorales, folk songs and dances, and composed pieces of definitely superior quality. But instead, what do we find to be the usual practice? In the best of situations the training of the beginner is continued, either in classes or by means of individual instruction, until he is capable of playing a part in a fairly advanced group. Even under the most favorable circumstances this transition is somewhat abrupt and he may experience some difficulties at first, but soon he acquires the necessary skill in ensemble playing and begins to feel that he belongs to the organization. Too often, however, the director is compelled by circumstances to admit all or most of his beginning players before they are quite ready, and this makes it advisable to use music which is below the level of the more advanced players. The process of absorbing new and inexperienced players goes on more or less continuously, with the result that a consistently low technical and musical level is imposed upon the entire organization, not for short periods but year after year. In consequence, little work of a progressive nature can be undertaken, and each season sees a repetition of the same process and the use of about the same standard of material.

This condition has played a large part in establishing the popularity of marches and easy overtures as basic training material, a trend which should be resisted by every possible means. Street marches, and to a lesser extent the easy overtures, lack variety of musical form and expression and emphasize the least desirable elements in performance. The melodic material upon which they are based is usually trite and repetitious, the phrases are short, the development of thematic material is limited, and little attention is given to matters of phrasing and dynamic change. The utility of this kind of music rests largely upon its diatonic nature, its reliance upon a few easy keys, and a lavish "doubling" in arrangement which gives the players confidence and insures that no essential part will be missing in performance. But what does the consistent use of this type of literature contribute to the development of the individual player? Actually, he is playing the same composition over and over under different titles and by different composers. He does not learn to read in the more extreme keys, he gains little knowledge of such meters as $\frac{3}{8}$, $\frac{9}{8}$, and $\frac{12}{8}$, his response to the niceties of phrasing is negligible, and any passage of a marked contrapuntal nature will most likely leave him completely baffled. These weaknesses, chiefly of a technical nature, might be corrected through the playing of more varied material and the use of more exacting methods of teaching.

Later in this text some attention will be given to problems of interpretation and the development of style in performance, matters which are of importance from the very start of a player's training. Unfortunately, this phase of teaching is usually neglected at the outset, with the result that many players never do receive any constructive help in interpretation. The matter is mentioned at this point because of its bearing upon the question of the choice of instructional materials. The library should include a great wealth of music selected primarily for its value in the cultivation of playing style — minuets, gavottes, waltzes, mazurkas, polonaises, barcarolles, fugues, folk songs, lyric pieces, and chorales. Ballet suites of the type of the *Pantomime* from *Il Cid* by Sacchini (published by Carl Fischer) are invaluable for this purpose, but for the most part the director will find it necessary to make his selection from the single numbers listed in the catalogues of various publishers.

Bands which have reached a fairly advanced stage in reading and playing ability will have access to a much wider choice of material than is available to beginning and intermediate organizations. All of this music is subject to limitations and criticisms which have already been mentioned, but at least it bears a resemblance to good music and gives promise of improvements to come. The most glaring faults spring from attempts to transcribe for band, compositions which are essentially in the idiom of the orchestra. For example, any attempt to arrange the Prelude to Act I of *Lohengrin,* with its whispering violin harmonics, is doomed to failure at the outset. This idiom simply cannot be carried over into the band. Any number in which the glide of a string portamento or certain special types of bowing supply the characteristic feature should be avoided, especially if the number is extremely well-known and loved in its original form. One who knows intimately the orchestral versions of the symphonic literature can never be happy in conducting, or even in hearing, band transcriptions of these same numbers. Perhaps, for their own peace of mind, it is just as well that many of our band conductors are not too familiar with the standard orchestral literature. The exceptions to the rule that orchestral compositions do not transcribe well for band probably prove that such numbers should have been written for band in the first place. While the number of such examples is not large, there are enough to suggest that a better technique of arranging for band might justify the permanent transfer of a good many standard compositions to the field of idiomatic band literature.

· Certain types of piano literature transcribe extremely well for band. An almost untouched field, and one which should prove eminently successful because of the similarity of the basic tonal media, is that of organ literature. This is the field which ambitious arrangers for band would do well to investigate, not only because of the natural relationship existing between organ and band but also because of the fact that the organ literature is not sufficiently well-known to arouse prejudice against the transcription as is frequently the case when favorite orchestral numbers are transcribed for band. Some of the best and most interesting transcriptions for band are those of the Bach *Preludes* and *Fugues* and certain of the Wagner excerpts. The latter are not uniformly good and must be approached with discrimination.

No attempt has been made to list specific numbers which might be suitable for use by orchestras and bands of different grades. Any such list would be far too lengthy for a work of this nature, and it would duplicate contributions which have already been made by other agencies. It must always remain for the conductor himself to determine what is suitable for his organizations and what is musically good according to his own standards.

CHAPTER VII

Editing of Scores and Parts

If by any chance the reader should add up the time required for the teacher to do all of the things which have already been outlined as being more or less essential to success, he will probably discover that all of the twenty-four hours of each day have been preempted. Such is the life of the teacher of instrumental music in the usual school situation, and not infrequently he is expected to teach academic courses and assume especial responsibilities in fields other than music in addition to the manifold extra-curricular activities directly associated with the music program.

Not the least of these "incidental" tasks is that of the revision and editing of at least a part of the music which his orchestra or band plays. The purposes of this revision are varied but have chiefly to do with the objective of securing a more satisfactory musical performance from groups of players which, as units, are not wholly adequate for the task at hand. Almost no group of amateur players is perfectly adapted to the performance of a musical work which has been arranged on the assumption that all players would be possessed of equal ability. Hence it is necessary to reenforce certain parts, transfer other portions from one section to another, lighten the accompaniment in some places, or supply an entirely new part for an instrument (such as the baritone horn in the orchestra) for which no printed part is supplied. In this type of revision the reference is chiefly to the smaller and less complete groups. As the instrumentation approaches final completeness the number of alterations required becomes fewer, but there always remains a considerable amount of work of this type to be done. Especially is this true with reference to band music because of the wide divergence in instrumentation and the inadequacies of so many of the published arrangements. Any orchestra which is complete and well-balanced will be able to play standard arrangements with little or no revision.

All of these changes are predicated upon one important consideration which a great many otherwise competent conductors seem to have overlooked. This is that every part or voice which the composer originally wrote into the work must be present in the final performance. If a particular instrument is missing from the ensemble, then the principal melodies and harmonies for this instrument must be written into the part for another instrument, retaining as nearly as possible the intended tone color and style and keeping within the proper register. The arrangements used by small orchestras and bands are most likely to require this sort of remedial writing, but for some unaccountable reason the conductors of such groups seem most inclined to ignore the matter entirely or to minimize its importance. Many teachers and conductors have never, from the beginning of their professional experience, rearranged a printed edition or made any adjustment in the parts.

In the smaller organizations the most common need is to supply parts for instruments which are not represented in the ensemble — usually oboe, bassoon, one or more horn parts, or even viola in the orchestra; and in the band, some of these same instruments plus alto or bass clarinet, E-flat clarinet, or perhaps one or more saxophones. Substitutions are never very satisfactory, but at least they represent an improvement over an incomplete harmonic structure and the complete absence of essential melodic material. Some of the generally accepted substitutions are: muted cornet or trumpet for oboe; baritone horn or trombone, tenor or baritone saxophone or even cello for bassoon; alto saxophone or muted trombone for horn (neither very satisfactory); clarinet or alto saxophone for melodic viola parts (the same for alto or bass clarinets in the band); and flutes for E-flat clarinet. The substitution will depend upon the nature and register of the part to be replaced, the exact tone color desired, the "weight" of accompanying parts, and the skill of the player who is to play the substitute part. In the use of muted instruments to represent other instruments, the type of mute used may determine the effectiveness of the substitution.

In addition to writing new parts for instruments which are not present in the ensemble, the conductor must also consider the problem of reenforcing those single instruments or sections which are tonally too weak to be effective in important passages. For example, the cello part can be strengthened by adding baritone horn, trombone, saxophone, or even low violin tone; or certain viola parts may be helped by the addition of either cello or violin. Occasionally it may be possible to improve the cello part by adding the string bass in octaves. In general, the same instruments which would be used as substitutes will serve quite adequately in the capacity of reenforcing instruments, but — and this is a most important point in rehearsal technique — the intended instrument must predominate over any added instruments in order to supply the proper tone color and style. This is best achieved by insisting that the players of supporting instruments always play a shade softer than the principal instrument. If they cannot hear the principal instrument as they play with it, it is a fair indication that they are playing too loudly.

Another type of re-marking which is helpful in saving rehearsal time is that concerned with dynamics. One of the great unsolved mysteries surrounding the whole field of composition, arranging, and editing is the manner in which the dynamic indications are used. In most published music the dynamic indications do not vary perpendicularly; that is, any given indication applies equally to all parts in the score from top to bottom. The only dynamic contrast called for in these editions is one which is horizontal, a progressive change in dynamics at various points in the composition. In other words, dynamic contrast between one portion of the piece and another is regarded as important, while dynamic differentiations between instruments or sections in the ensemble are unimportant. The indication *ff*, for example, means that all are to play *ff*; whereas, to secure the desired balance of parts it is necessary that certain instruments play *ff*, others *f*, and still others *mf*.

The traditional but nevertheless faulty and inaccurate practice outlined above places the greatest imaginable obstacles in the way of both conductor and students. A very large portion of the rehearsal time may be required to "break down" the dynamic differentiations in order that proper balance between sections, proper harmonic coloring, and proper relationships between melody and accompaniment may be secured. A device adopted by many conductors is that of asking the players to interpret any given dynamic marking one degree louder if the part is melodic and one degree softer if it is accompaniment. This tends to make the players more alert to discover what is the most important musical material, but it is too variable a practice and it still does not solve the problem entirely. The only safe procedure to follow, especially in the case of compositions being prepared for concerts or contests, is for the conductor to edit the dynamic indications in terms of the numerical balance of his sections and the ability of individual players.

Most amateur organizations will have more than one player assigned to each of the separate wind parts as, in fact, do most professional organizations. This is especially desirable in the case of school orchestras and bands as it insures a complete balance at all times and helps in the development of the younger and less experienced players who usually fill the "second" chairs. It is understood in all professional organizations that only the first player at each stand is to play when the passage calls for a solo part, a duet between two instruments, or any very light combination of instruments in which intonation and delicate ensemble are major considerations. This commonly accepted practice is based upon the very sound theory that no two instruments of a kind can play absolutely in unison in matters of pitch, tone quality, attack and release, dynamic variation, and articulation. There must always be, even among the most skillful players, a slight variation in these details which would destroy a perfect ensemble. This safe and desirable method has been adopted by all professional orchestras and bands but not, unfortunately, by most of the amateur organizations. In all *tutti* passages, of course, the entire ensemble participates.

Assuming that the amateur group will wish to follow the "no doubling" rule stated above, the conductor must indicate in all parts the passages which are to be played solo and those which are to be doubled. These changes may be marked simply by bracketing with a colored pencil the portions which are to be played only by the first player at each stand.

Still another phase of the editing which is required of the conductor deals with the simplification of parts to bring them within the limits of the players' abilities. If a given passage in sixteenth notes is too difficult it can sometimes be rewritten in eighth notes (omitting each alternate sixteenth) without serious loss of musical effectiveness. This method of simplification is usually applied to an accompanying or "filler" part, the principal function of which is to supply a background of harmony with an added touch of motion.

Occasionally this type of part can be treated somewhat differently to preserve more nearly its original pattern. This method involves dividing a violin or clarinet section into several sub-sections as suggested by the following:

In some instances a passage which is extremely difficult for one group of players may be relatively easy for instruments of a different type, and in these cases it is quite legitimate to reenforce the difficult part so that it may be produced effectively. This practice is not advised in dealing with the classic or standard literature, but it has its place in the program of developing amateur players. Occasionally, if applied with discretion, the same principle may be utilized with large and well-balanced groups playing standard compositions. A good example occurs in the Liszt *Les Preludes* where the second violins have a scale passage which is followed by an answering scale passage by the first violins. The two sections alternate in this manner for a matter of twelve measures. These runs always lack both volume and clarity when played by amateurs; but by combining the parts into a continuous scale passage played by both sections simultaneously a very satisfactory effect is produced, especially if sufficient accent can be applied to the first note of each run. This type of corrective rewriting pays big dividends in the final performance, but it requires careful study of the scores and cautious handling to preserve the original intent of the composer.

Not the least of the advance work on the scores and parts of orchestral material must go into the marking of fingerings and bowings. Upon the choice of fingerings especially may the success of the string sections be said to depend, because, as was mentioned in an earlier chapter, certain passages which would be practically unplayable in one position or with a given sequence of fingerings may be executed easily and naturally through a slightly different approach. Furthermore, the question of tone quality must be considered. Each string has its own tonal characteristics, and these differences in quality should be utilized in giving special significance to the various types of melodies and harmonies. Sometimes a part will be so fingered as to stress the portamento, or sliding effect, which is only possible on the strings and the trombone. There are literally hundreds of minor possibilities presented in the most ordinary string part, and the correct choice will often be determined by the "feel" of the passage to the player. This, in turn, explains the tremendous advantage which the string-trained orchestra conductor enjoys over one who must apply a textbook or second-hand knowledge to the solution of string problems. In marking the string fingerings the conductor must constantly keep in mind the technical limitations of his players, and his choices may frequently represent a compromise between what is best and what is possible.

In the matter of bowing, the considerations are much the same — a determination of method based upon joint problems of technique and musical effectiveness; but in addition there is the special matter of uniformity. The players within a section may not always use the same fingerings, but their bowing should be as uniform as possible. This is partly for the sake of appearance, but it is mainly to insure maximum clarity in all fundamental matters — attack, rhythm, volume control, and style.

Few conductors can find the necessary time to mark all of the string parts, but at least one of each should be marked for the use of the principals in the sections. These should be clearly labelled "Marked Copy" and should be available for reference. If the players themselves do not have time to mark their own parts from the master copies, they should observe the rule: When in doubt, follow the principal in your section. The best procedure for the conductor to follow is to mark all bowings and fingerings in the full score, if one is available, as this permits him to see the relationship between the various parts. Where there is any similarity between two or more parts they should be fingered or bowed uniformly. In the absence of specific bowing indications all principals will follow the lead of the concertmaster or the principal of the next section in order. For example, where all string parts are alike in rhythm and bowing all will adopt the bowing set by the concertmaster, but if only the second violins and the violas have like bowing, the principal second violin player will establish the pattern for both sections. Where the string sections are entirely independent the principal of each will determine the bowing to be used within his section.

The editing of band scores and parts frequently presents a major problem in arranging. This is principally due to the disorganized state of band instrumentation to which a general reference was made in another chapter. The earlier American editions did not include saxophone parts, much less alto and bass clarinet parts. In recent years these parts have been added — superimposed upon an already supposedly complete arrangement. These early editions did have E-flat cornet parts and sometimes tenor horn parts. What happens to these voices in the modern band? The older arrangements provided E-flat clarinet parts and frequently piccolo parts, but often none for flute. Many of them included only two or three horn (alto) parts and these were written, of course, for the E-flat instrument. The trombone parts in treble clef and the E-flat bass parts of these older editions are of still less use to the modern band. Some later editions contained saxophone parts (including one for the B-flat soprano) but no parts for alto and bass clarinet. Few of the older editions provided for the use of tympani.

No less confusing is the problem presented by even the more recent foreign editions, some of which provide only two cornet parts and others of which include a complete series of Saxhorn parts in various keys and registers in addition to numerous other instruments, the identity of which many conductors can only guess. A band library of any size will contain the most fantastically varied assortment of editions, including music for every conceivable combination of wind instruments, arranged according to all possible systems of instrumentation. It becomes the task of the conductor to bring order out of this chaos by a complicated process of redistribution, elimination, substitution, transposition, and other forms of legerdemain. How peaceful to conduct the orchestra with its fixed balance of parts, its firmly established science of instrumentation, and its great body of dependable literature!

This work is not designed as a textbook on instrumentation and hence it is impossible to delve deeply into the problem of editing and revising band scores. The terms "editing" and "revision" are, in fact, grossly misleading. What is necessary in a great many cases is the complete rewriting of the works in question. The situation is something like this: some bands have BB-flat basses, others have E-flat basses, and many have both. Therefore, the printed bass part must be a compromise, a combination which is correct for neither but which can be played (in a manner of speaking) by either or both. For bands that do not have alto and bass clarinets, important parts for these instruments should be given to saxophones. The plan works admirably for those bands which have one or the other, but it works very badly for those which happen to have both. Or, consider the case of the fluegelhorn, to which should be assigned a special and characteristic type of melody. In case the band does not have a fluegelhorn the melodies for this instrument must be written into the parts for other instruments, say the cornet or the trumpet. This is a splendid idea for those bands which do not have fluegelhorns; but if the arrangement is played by a complete band, there is again the doubling of voices which do not blend, and the musical effect is lost.

Endless examples might be cited to illustrate the deficiencies of available band arrangements from an artistic standpoint. There have been marked improvements as a direct result of pressure brought to bear by such organizations as the American Bandmasters Association, and it is to be hoped that the publishers will continue to cooperate with the profession in these matters. If the bandsmen themselves would now turn their attention from matters of instrumentation and the number of parts to be provided by the publishers to the equally vital problem of securing the publication of worthwhile compositions, properly arranged, the lot of band conductors who are also musicians would be made somewhat easier.

Until some further progress is made in these matters the conductor will be compelled to do what is possible in the way of a superfical editing of the band parts. This will involve the "thinning out" of certain portions, the enrichment of others by lowering the bass parts and filling in the middle registers with more carefully written bassoon, alto and bass clarinet parts, and the "mellowing" of the top register by substituting a body of flutes for the E-flat and higher B-flat clarinets. In general, the high brass should be toned down in volume and should be treated more in the manner of the orchestra trumpets, except for essentially melodic parts; and for certain of these melodies the fluegelhorns should be used almost exclusively.

Treatment of the general subject of the editorial revision of published band and orchestra music would be incomplete without some mention of the need of inserting rehearsal letters or numbers in the editions in which these markings have been omitted. No amateur group can be expected to play completely through a composition without occasional interruptions for corrections or suggestions affecting the performance. If these stops occur, however, in the middle of a long composition which contains no rehearsal letters or numbers, the resulting confusion and loss of time present a major problem in rehearsal management. Should the conductor attempt to establish a common starting point by reference to dynamic indications or other musical landmarks, the results would probably be unsatisfactory and, in the end, the only possible solution would be to start again at the beginning or to count innumerable measures from some well-understood break in the composition. In either case valuable time would be wasted, interest in the performance would be dissipated, and the original purpose for which the playing was halted would likely be forgotten. After a few experiences of this kind the wise conductor will either swear never again to use music which does not contain rehearsal letters or numbers, or he will devote a considerable portion of his remaining free time to inserting the markings in individual parts. Happily, most modern editions are well supplied with these important indications, but most libraries still contain many numbers from which they have been omitted.

Many conductors of school orchestras and bands will take the position that the final results are insufficient to justify the expenditure of time and effort required for the revisions which have been suggested. In support of their position they may argue that the arrangements were made originally by experts and approved by editorial supervisors who must have been familiar with the practical problems of the music classroom. This may be an erroneous assumption. The fact that an arrangement is available in printed form, or that a given statement appears in a book, is no assurance of its reliability. Books are written and music is composed or arranged by men whose knowledge and experience may be either broad or narrow and whose ideas may be either true or false. It is for the reader or the musician to determine whether these ideas or practices apply in his particular situation. In the case of the arranger of instrumental music, one should inquire whether he is a truly skillful arranger, whether he is guided by the dictates of real artistry (which implies a background of culture and art knowledge), whether he has ever taught amateur musicians under ordinary school conditions, and whether he is free to make his arrangements as he knows they should be made. The conductor's contribution to the cause must be to use more discrimination in his selection of music materials.

CHAPTER VIII

Stringed Instruments

At various points in preceding chapters the more general qualifications of the music teacher and the conductor have been enumerated. These qualifications have included musicianship, cultural background, technical training, professional experience, attitude toward teaching, and understanding of children; but up to this point no special emphasis has been placed upon a factor which is, in the last analysis, perhaps of greater imporance than any other. This is the ability to "draw out of a hat," like the magician of old, an inexhaustible supply of technical and musical minutiae with which to meet any situation that might arise.

In the early days of public school instrumental music it was deemed quite sufficient if the orchestra "leader" knew the names of the various instruments and could recognize most of them by sight. If he happened to know how to finger the C scale on the cornet and the G scale on the violin (without half-steps!), he was regarded as being extremely well-qualified. More than one young teacher has found it necessary to keep at least one day ahead of his classes on certain instruments, but this was before the day of clinics, demonstrations, comprehensive instrumental courses in teacher-training institutions, and "fool-proof" instrumental methods. If the early teacher knew one or two instruments thoroughly upon entering the profession, he was fortunate indeed, but like most beginning teachers he usually learned rapidly.

It is one thing to be able to play an instrument well, or even to have a thorough understanding of all of the technical problems involved in its playing, but it is quite a different thing to have this ability and knowledge so organized as to be able to present it, one idea at a time, to young players who cannot absorb the matter in any other way. The oft-repeated saying, "Teachers are born, not made," is as true today as it ever was. Many there are who might have been born teachers but who have failed to achieve their destiny because they did not possess a complete and detailed knowledge of their subject-matter. To say, "Do as I do!" is not good teaching procedure, although it certainly does have its place in teaching technique. The teaching of any subject which is based so largely upon the acquisition of fixed skills must include a certain amount of drill and physical discipline *per se,* but the most adroit pedagogue will probably combine the two essential features — explanation and drill — in order that the act may be supported by the intellect.

To present a complete outline of the technical problems involved in the playing of the various instruments would be quite beyond the scope of this work even if it were within the capacity of the writer to compile such an imposing body of information. There are, however, a few facts about the instruments themselves, the manner of playing them, and the techniques of presenting some of the fundamental problems related to them, that seem worthy of inclusion in a text of this type. These facts and theories are certainly not to be regarded as indisputable, conclusive, or in any sense comprehensive. They are intended only to suggest a basis of approach for such teachers as may not have a practical knowledge of all of the various instruments.

Perhaps the most common cause of the failure and half-success of so many school orchestra and band conductors is their inability to appreciate the importance of fundamentals in their teaching. The ex-professional musician has advanced so far beyond these elementary considerations in his own work that he cannot remember their importance, and the non-professional *teacher*-conductor has perhaps never fully understood them. There is no substitute for the complete mastery of those few elements which govern the production of good tone, the control of variations in tone (volume and quality), accuracy of intonation, facility of execution, and contrast in playing style. A great many teachers, and most of the listening public, seem to be under the impression that there is some sort of magic in the act of converting a nondescript assemblage of poorly-taught instrumentalists into a balanced and efficient orchestra or band capable of executing and interpreting the easier masterworks. To any who have proved their ability to take over almost any kind of a group and develop that group into a satisfactory playing combination, there is no magic in the process; there is only hard work and attention to the details of mechanics and interpretation.

There is a belief, quite firmly established in some quarters, that interpretation as such cannot be either taught or learned — that one either has it or he doesn't have it. This view was once expressed by a very famous violin teacher with reference to the vibrato. Such expressions reflect an attitude which is fatal to good teaching and which cannot be defended in the light of the splendid results which have been and are being achieved with very ordinary artistic raw material. It would be equally false to believe or to assert that all aspiring young musicians have the capacity to attain the absolute heights, either technically or musically. Some will reach the saturation point earlier than others, but this saturation point is not absolutely fixed for all individuals in the group; it is controlled to a very large extent by the inspirational qualities and the teaching skill of the conductor.

On the mechanical side of performance it is important that the teacher be able to inspire enthusiasm and ambition, but the more practical considerations of cause and effect will apply with special force in this category. All that most young people demand is proof that what the teacher says is true. They are, in a sense, skeptics. They must be convinced that a given line of reasoning is logical and that whatever they may be told to do is essential and will produce the desired results. Once the instrumental teacher has established a general belief that the technical devices which he seeks to employ will make a definite and specific contribution to the improvement of the performance, he will have won the confidence of his players and he will enjoy a comparatively free hand in the application of corrective techniques and supplementary drill processes.

The very first of the purely mechanical problems to be solved is that of keeping the instruments in satisfactory playing condition, and upon the teacher's success in this matter everything else may depend. A simple and direct question will serve to emphasize the importance of this single item to the ultimate musical success of the organization: If a skilled professional player could not produce satisfactory results upon the instrument in question, what may be expected from an inexperienced, partially-trained, and none-too-resourceful amateur on the same instrument? This idea may be impressed upon the student player whose instrument is not in playable condition by stating it somewhat more simply: Even Fritz Kreisler would have some difficulty in playing this instrument!

The players of the brass instruments experience the least difficulty in keeping their playing equipment in good order, the problems of the percussionist are not insurmountable, the woodwind players must be constantly on the alert for mechanical deficiencies, but the players of the stringed instruments face a problem of real magnitude. Unfortunately, there are few skilled string repairmen available to provide the necessary service. Minor adjustments can be made by teachers or others, provided they understand the work thoroughly and have a few special tools; but major repairs should be undertaken only by an expert. Most of the mechanical deficiencies which interfere with the proper playing of the stringed instruments are of a fairly minor nature, but their importance in the aggregate cannot be overestimated. The more important of these matters are listed here as a basis for any general check-up which the teacher might wish to institute within his own organization:

1. Cracks and openings in the body of the instrument, or loose linings within.

2. Poorly-fitted pegs and improperly spaced string-holes in the pegs.

3. Warped or "rutted" fingerboard.

4. Head-nut too low or too high.

5. Poorly-trimmed and poorly-fitted bridge.

6. Warped bow or one needing refilling.

7. Worn or broken frog mechanism on bow.

(All of the above items will probably require the attention of a skilled repairman.)

8. Poor quality or wrong-type strings. The almost universally accepted stringing of the violin is as follows: steel E (with screw tuning-device on tailpiece), gut A, aluminum-wrapped gut D, silver-wrapped gut G. The following strings are recommended for the viola and the cello: gut A and D, silver or copper G and C; and for the bass: gut G and D, copper A and E. Some players may prefer other types of strings, but the best results will be obtained by using as many gut strings, or strings wound with metal on gut, as possible. The all-metal strings tend toward hardness of tone and should be used with discretion. The important matter is, however, that all strings be of good quality and in good condition.

9. Accessories. The following accessories are recommended: Good chin-rests for violins and violas, preferably the type which

clamps over the end-block of the instrument; shoulder-pads for all violinists and violists (the advice of the Auer school of instruction notwithstanding); adjustable end-pins and end-pin rests for cellists; extra strings, mutes, and rosin available at all times.

10. Cases. All instruments should, of course, be carried and stored in substantial cases which provide maximum protection against damage, moisture, and temperature changes.

To secure and maintain a satisfactory level in this matter of proper conditioning of the stringed instruments will require constant observation on the part of the conductor and no little care and expense on the part of the players, but in the end it will prove its value to the organization. A very definite improvement in both technical facility and in tone invariably follows a general check-up where these matters have been neglected, and still more important, the players will enjoy their work much more when they are not compelled to fight against purely mechanical obstacles.

The conductor will not hope to complete the conditioning of the instruments before proceeding with other matters, as this is a continuing process, one which will require attention as long as orchestras and bands exist. To impress upon the players the importance of the proper adjustment of their instruments the conductor should illustrate freely in rehearsal the unsatisfactory results which come from faulty instruments or lack of uniformity in equipment. A warped or rutted violin fingerboard, or a head-nut or bridge which is too low, will cause the string to vibrate against the fingerboard, producing a raucous noise. This is most noticeable in loud playing when the pressure of the bow depresses the string. A single illustration of this mechanical defect will serve a valuable purpose. To illustrate the harm which may be caused by a bridge which is too flat across the top, it is suggested that the teacher attempt to play on the A or the D string with maximum bow pressure. The bow cannot fail to come in contact with the two adjacent strings and thus sound three strings instead of the one intended. Even the effect of poor strings may be illustrated, but not as effectively as the mechanical defects already mentioned. Another useful device is to have the violin section play a given passage with mutes, then to repeat the passage with half of the instruments muted and half without mutes. A few repetitions will show the importance of having a completely muted section where this is desired. As a matter of emphasis on this point, no player should be permitted to play muted passages unless he has a mute. One final suggestion concerns the use of chin-rests and shoulder-pads. Players who think that they can do without these items should be asked to experiment with other instruments equipped with different types of chin-rests and shoulder-pads until they find the type which suits them and facilitates the support of the instrument. This is most important since no player can concentrate upon his playing if most of his attention is being diverted to the problem of holding the instrument in position.

No less mechanical in their fundamentals are the problems of posture, tone production, and technique. Without attempting to go deeply into these matters, it might be helpful to discuss a few of the most important considerations, especially those which may have a direct bearing upon group performance.

The bodily posture of all players in an orchestra or band should be comfortably erect — not stiff, not rigid, not tense or strained, but not careless or slouchy. The instruments should be held correctly, after the pattern of the best professional (not dance band) players, and there should be a reasonable degree of uniformity in this respect. A good general rule affecting the disposition of the feet and legs — always something of a problem in younger groups — is "a toe near a heel." If this rule is followed, an extremely awkward position is quite impossible. The cello and string bass players will, of course, disregard the rule. In this connection it might be well to emphasize the importance of seating the organization in more or less exact semicircles, with every player facing directly toward the conductor.

The production of tone on a stringed instrument is a fairly simple problem in theory, but it seems to present major difficulties in practice. Possibly a better general understanding of the theory would improve the practice. Fundamentally, these are the mechanical requirements: 1. The bow should be held with a degree of relaxed control which will permit variations in the speed and the pressure of the bow movement. 2. The control of the bow should be such that it remains effective at the extremities as well as in the middle portion. 3. The bow should be drawn at right angles to the string and either near to the bridge or over the end of the fingerboard as may be dictated by the nature of the tone or the volume desired. 4. Changes in the direction of the bow should be executed smoothly and without loss of volume or quality of tone. 5. The player's hold upon the bow-stick should be such that he can lift the bow from the string and replace it without materially affecting the immediate and subsequent manipulation in the manner already described.

These various factors in bow control account for the practically unlimited variation which is possible in tone quality and expression on the stringed instruments. A slowly-drawn bow with a maximum amount of pressure will produce quite a different quality of tone from that produced by a quickly-drawn stroke with a minimum amount of pressure. Added to these many possible variants there are hundreds more which are determined by the distance of the bow from the bridge, and to these must be added still more possibilities resulting from fingering changes, i.e., whether a given tone is played upon one string or another and the length of the vibrating portion of the string. These somewhat technical considerations are mentioned here only to suggest some of the reasons for tonal differences in the stringed instruments. For all practical purposes it is only necessary for the player to remember and practice the bare fundamentals enumerated above, principally to develop a reasonably satisfactory relationship between bow-speed and bow-pressure and sufficient control to keep the bow at the correct angle and in the right place on the string.

The matter of lifting the bow is essential. There are literally thousands of amateur string players who never lift the bow from the strings, chiefly because they have formed the habit of utilizing the bow-on-string contact as a control factor. To lift the bow from the string involves the risk of dropping it, and the unskilled player exercises discretion in this matter even though he be deprived thereby of one of the chief means of obtaining contrast in his playing. The bouncing-bow and the lifted-bow techniques are vital to any adequate string performance and they are the principal source of variety in orchestral style; but countless amateur groups have never availed themselves of this added interest. This is but one of many instances which illustrate the close relationship which must always exist between musical expression and an adequate understanding of technical groundwork.

Before leaving this question of the lifted- and bouncing-bow techniques, the common distinctions between them should be further clarified. The lifted, or "carried," bow-stroke may be very short or of considerable length, but its use is usually restricted to the lower half of the bow. Above the middle it becomes more difficult to control the bow action. The lifted stroke is definitely a controlled action but it may merge into a more flexibly executed single-bounce stroke which is a form of the spiccato, sometimes referred to as a controlled spiccato stroke. The natural spiccato implies a quicker sequence of very short bounces controlled in groups or, as in the case of a "bow tremolo," a very rapid succession of semi-bouncing strokes. No one but a string player can appreciate all of the modifications of these various fundamental bowings, but the conductor should at least try to acquire a working knowledge of the more common types.

A third basic form of bowing (the first two being the sustained and the lifted or bouncing bow) is the staccato. This stroke is characterized by its special form of attack and its sudden stop, whether the actual stroke be short or long, single down-and-up, or a series of strokes in the same direction. The chief distinguishing factor is the "prepared attack," although in a rapid series of staccato tones this attack is so slight as to almost escape observation. In executing the stroke the bow is held stationary on the string and a definite pressure is applied to the string by the bow. At the instant of starting the stroke this pressure is suddenly released and this double action gives the tone that peculiar "snap" which distinguishes it from all other bow-strokes. The identical technique is applied to all forms of short and long accented and detached strokes, and since these usually follow in some kind of a sequence, the abrupt stopping of the motion of the bow is in the nature of a preparation for the staccato stroke which is to follow. One of the interesting variations of this stroke is its application at the start of a sustained bow-stroke, giving the effect of a *fp*.

The left-hand technique of the string player is one of the determining factors in the intonation of the orchestra, and this is a problem which requires the most careful study and unceasing vigilance on the part of the conductor at every rehearsal. A correct left-hand technique is based upon three elements: a thorough understanding of the principle of fingering patterns in their relationship to the actual notes to be played, practiced skill in the use of these patterns, and a discriminating sense of pitch. Pitch sense has been named last for a considered reason, which is this: if a player depends largely or entirely upon a keen ear, he will form the habit of depending upon the ear instead of upon the muscular "feel" of the finger relationships. Theoretically, at least, the player who plays "by ear" may play each note twice, first wrong and then right. Actually, an orchestral player is not always able to distinguish the exact pitch of the tone which he himself plays, but in any case he must know by his kinesthetic and tactile senses *before* he sounds the tone that it will be correct. The only way that this can be done by the string player is through a highly developed sense of finger relationships based upon fundamental patterns and positions, with certain prescribed variations.

This system of patterns is best illustrated by the following note sequences to be played on the D string of the violin:

These ten patterns cover all of the common finger relationships and at least one (J) which is rarely used. An interesting parlor game might be based upon the use of these patterns, the idea being to locate as many as possible of the patterns in the major and minor scales. For example, sequence B is the lower tetrachord of the E major scale and the upper tetrachord of the A major scale, sequence E is the upper tetrachord of the A harmonic minor scale, and sequence F is the lower tetrachord of the E-flat minor scale, while sequence K is a part of the F minor scale. To the violinist this is much more than a parlor game — it is the heart of his left-hand technique, and upon his ability to see these note sequences as fingering patterns will depend much of his accuracy in intonation and his facility in reading and execution. In order to fix the correct fingering habits in mind and muscle he should exaggerate the "closeness" of the half-steps and the "farness" of the whole-steps. The human hand is not built for violin technique, the natural spacing of the fingers being something between a half-step and a whole-step. But our musical scale

is not based upon a three-quarter tone! A great many school orchestras regularly play a three-quarter tone interval, but this does
not improve the clarity and resonance of the ensemble performance.

Carrying the technical basis of the left hand a bit farther, the
four fundamental types of finger movement should be mentioned,
and these four types of action should be practiced as such. There is
the *perpendicular*, or up-and-down, movement of the finger as illustrated by the simple trill. Next in difficulty is the *longitudinal* movement of the finger as found in the chromatic shift. The *lateral* shift
involves moving a finger from one string to an exactly corresponding position on another string, and finally, the *diagonal* shift requires
the movement of a finger to a position one half-step higher or lower,
on an adjacent string. The last of these — the difficult diagonal shift
— accounts for a large share of the faulty intonation in the string
sections of our orchestras. Following are some simple exercises which
illustrate these four basic types of finger movement:

In the foregoing paragraphs only the most basic elements of
string technique have been discussed. It would be quite impossible
to go into detail concerning all of the hundreds of technical problems involved in the playing of the stringed instruments, but those
which have been mentioned briefly may at least help the conductor
to improve the bowing and fingering of his violinists and other
string players. The viola technique is essentially the same as that of
the violin. The cello technique is the same in principle except that
the basic fingering pattern for the diatonic scales in first position
utilizes a 1st-3rd-4th, or a 1st-2nd-4th finger sequence wherever a
half-step is involved. For the extended reaches used in playing adjacent whole-step progressions, a 1st-2nd-4th finger pattern is employed, the first finger being extended backward or the fourth upward as the situation might require.

The string bass utilizes, in the elementary stages, a fingering system based upon chromatic progressions in either "half-position" or "first-position." A series of three chromatic progressions is played with the first, second, and fourth fingers, with the third finger supporting the fourth. A more extensive use of the higher positions is essential to the bass player, as well as to the cello player, who goes beyond the very beginning stages. In fact, a knowledge of positions should be stressed at a fairly early stage for violin and viola players as well.

The principal danger in undertaking to present so limited a resumé of the technical problems of any group of instruments is that the reader may regard the treatment as adequate for his immediate needs or criticize the author for not covering the ground more thoroughly. In this case the chief purpose has been to emphasize some points concerning which little mention has been made in most published methods and to present these items in a form in which they may be of some direct and practical aid to the orchestral conductor. He should, in any case, go directly to the standard instruction books or, better still, to a competent private teacher for a complete and thorough grounding in the technique of these instruments.

CHAPTER IX

Woodwind Instruments

Of the four main bodies of instruments the strings are the most homogeneous in character. If we exclude the harp and the piano, which are not classified with the bowed stringed instruments, the quality of tone throughout the entire string range is fundamentally the same for all instruments, and the basic technique does not vary except in relatively minor details. This fact probably explains the general acceptance of the string body as the tonal basis of the orchestra, although other contributing factors must be recognized — the comparatively early perfection of stringed instrument construction, the extreme flexibility of execution which is possible on the stringed instruments, the fact that most listeners can tolerate string tone for extended periods of time, and perhaps most important of all, the endurance of the players themselves. The playing of a stringed instrument does not involve the vital bodily function of breathing, nor is the tone actually produced by a part of the body as in the case of the brass player whose lips must withstand constant vibration and contact with a mouthpiece. These fundamental differences between the strings and the winds must always be taken into account in dealing with the technical and musical problems of the various sections.

The woodwind instruments are generally supposed to serve a function in the band comparable to that of the strings in the orchestra, but in view of the fundamental differences mentioned in the preceding paragraph this is not entirely possible. Not only do the woodwind instruments fall short in the matter of range, but they also lack uniformity in tone color both as between instruments of different types and even within the range of any one. To illustrate this point further, there is considerably more difference between the tone of the bassoon, saxophones, alto and bass clarinets, B-flat clarinet, oboe, flute, and piccolo than there is between the tone of the string bass, cello, viola, and violin. There is also the marked difference within the range of the B-flat clarinet itself, as represented by the chalumeau, throat, clarion, and high registers, each of which has a character quite distinct from that of the others.

In the orchestra, this wide variation in woodwind tone color serves a most useful purpose in providing an element of contrast which is greatly needed to enrich the ensemble tone. This contrasting quality has its use in the band also. The fact, however, that the band can claim no single group of instruments capable of supplying a consistent and uniform tonal background constitutes a rather serious handicap to the conductor in his efforts to build a truly balanced and homogeneous musical structure. It becomes a case of having to utilize a decorative and essentially variable substance in place of solid and uniform material of greater durability. This is a problem for which there does not seem to be any immediate general solution. In isolated cases in which the combination of the woodwind instruments lacks smoothness and integration, definite improvement may be effected by rearranging the parts and by giving the most detailed attention to such matters as tone production, tone control, intonation, and the blending of the various voices.

The importance of having the instruments always in the best of mechanical condition has already been emphasized in the case of the strings. Where the woodwind instruments are concerned, proper conditioning is even more vital to the production of satisfactory results because of the fact that even a small leak in the instrument may make it impossible to produce a sound of any kind in certain parts of the register. If such a leak does not shut off the tone entirely, it will usually be the cause of faulty intonation throughout the range of the instrument. Unsuitable or improperly trimmed reeds may have the same effect. Failure of the key mechanism may result from a number of causes, including broken, weak, or bent springs; twisted posts or key shafts; improper adjustment of pads, key-corking, or key mechanism buffers; key adjustment screws which are either too tight or too loose; or worn pads. In fact, there are perhaps more different ways in which a woodwind instrument can get out of adjustment than there are accidentals in an ultramodern composition, and they lead to almost as much confusion and bewilderment. As in the case of the strings, the safest procedure is to have the woodwind instruments inspected and reconditioned at reasonably frequent intervals by an expert repairman; but care in the handling of the instruments will reduce the cost and the inconvenience of such periodic checks.

If a woodwind instrument is poorly constructed or if it is built of poor materials, no amount of attention or expense will ever convert it into a usable instrument. Especially is this true in matters of pitch and intonation. If the bore of the instrument is faulty or if the tone-holes are improperly spaced, tinkering and adjusting will be of little avail, and both player and conductor will find the instrument a source of constant irritation. In the light of these facts, it is always advisable to purchase the best grade of standard-make instrument and to give the instrument the best possible care from the beginning.

Of all of the woodwind instruments the piccolo is the most flagrant offender in the matter of intonation, but fortunately, the type of part generally assigned to this instrument makes some allowance for its natural shortcomings. The piccolo seldom carries a sustained part, and usually it is employed merely to add a flash of piercing tonal brilliance to tutti passages. Any other use of the instrument should be discouraged by the conductor unless he happens to have an unusually fine instrument and a player who can manage it with consummate skill. It is a mistake to assume that every flutist can play the piccolo as it should be played. The proper execution of characteristic piccolo parts demands unusual facility of lips, tongue, and fingers and for the piccolo player in the band, the ability to make the ordinary transpositions from C to D-flat, and vice versa. The same skill in transposition is required of the flute player in the band since both C and D-flat flute parts are found in the ordinary band library, depending upon the edition and the arrangement. The best solution is to select players who can play all parts on the C instruments; an alternative but less satisfactory solution is to provide the players with flutes and piccolos in both keys.

The flutist probably has less mechanical difficulty with his instrument than any of the other woodwind players, probably because these instruments are made of metal and do not depend upon the use of a reed in the production of the tone. Almost the only fault in the adjustment of the instrument, excepting with reference to the spring, key, and pad mechanisms which are common to all woodwind instruments, is in the improper placement of the cork plug in the head-joint. This stopper must always be located exactly as specified by the manufacturer.

In addition to the matters of adjustment which have already been mentioned, the clarinet player's chief problems have to do with the choice of a mouthpiece and the selection of a suitable reed. It is common knowledge that a good mouthpiece and a good reed will overcome most of the faults of a clarinet except those arising from basically faulty construction or obviously poor adjustment of the key and pad mechanisms. Mouthpieces differ in the matter of the lay, or the facing, which is that part of the mouthpiece against which the reed is placed. This lay may be long or short, open or close; and in addition there are a great many special lays in which the angle or degree of curvature varies from the base to the tip. Specialists on the instrument will have their preferences, ranging from one extreme to the other and coupled with a preference in the strength and texture of the reed to be used with any given lay. While the use of special reeds for particular playing demands is a fairly common practice, many players even go to the length of using mouthpieces of different lays for different purposes. For most amateur players this degree of specialization in the use of equipment seems hardly necessary. A good safe practice is to try several medium types of mouthpieces and to select the one which seems to give the best results with the minimum amount of effort. Reeds should be chosen in much the same manner, by experimentation. Care should be exercised in the choice of reeds to insure proper balance between tone quality, ease of playing, and intonation, especially in the highest and the lowest registers.

All that has been said regarding the selection of mouthpieces and reeds applies with equal force to the alto and bass clarinets, and to the saxophones. Special attention should be given in the case of these larger instruments to the operation of the key mechanism. The increased size and weight of the keys on these instruments constitutes an added impediment to a rapid, flexible execution. The player himself must make every effort to overcome this handicap through the development of a facile technique.

The oboe, English horn, and bassoon players must face all of the mechanical hazards common to the other woodwind instruments and some others which are peculiar to the double reed group. Most of these special difficulties are in some manner related to the choice of reeds. The double reed is an extremely sensitive and unpredictable mechanical device. Its temperamental qualities have been demonstrated on many occasions, much to the chagrin and embarrassment of players who have had both the will and the skill to play their parts as intended. There is no positive remedy for the tonal instability of the double reeds — only a few suggestions which may or may not prove helpful. Reeds made by a professional for the profession are usually to be preferred, for they presumably will have been tested by one who actually plays the instrument. In general, it is best for students to use reeds which are not too stiff. Many failures to produce satisfactory tone may be traced to the use of reeds which are hard and inflexible. Keep the reed clean and dry when not in use but moisten the tip and the inside surface of the reed by drawing clear water through it a few minutes before each rehearsal or practice period. Much of the deterioration of the double reed results from the use of the reed before it has been sufficiently moistened.

As in the case of the strings, the woodwind instruments must be subjected to constant checking and re-checking to insure against some slight fault in adjustment which may affect the tone quality or the intonation of the entire ensemble. As much as one might wish to delegate the responsibility for this checking to the players of these instruments, it is the conductor himself who must assume the initiative and institute such general or individual inspections as may be necessary. The playing of the instruments will be difficult enough for the student, and the conductor's task of coordinating the various instruments will be sufficiently exacting, without either one having to face unnecessary obstacles in the form of poor equipment.

On the technical side there is much more in common between the instruments of various types than the student, and sometimes the conductor, may realize. In fact, this similarity in the technique of the instruments also carries over into the field of vocal music, especially as regards the process of breathing and breath control. Fortunate indeed is the band conductor whose organization includes a number of well-schooled vocalists and perhaps a still larger number of players who have had choral training under competent leadership, for the basic principles of choral and band work are much the same.

A superficial comparison of the technical bases of the stringed instruments and the woodwind instruments will show that they have these points in common: 1. TONE. For the strings, *the drawn bow*, with such variations as may be introduced by means of different types of bow manipulation. For the woodwind, *the breath*, with similar variations controlled by the tongue, lips, or reed. 2. PITCH. For the strings, *the left-hand technique.* For the woodwind, *the entire key mechanism.* In the case of the flute, and to a less marked degree the other woodwind instruments, the embouchure contributes to the pitch change also. This similarity in the physical process of playing instruments which appear to have little in common, is cited for the purpose of emphasizing the fact that all of the ordinary technical and expressive devices may be explained and dealt with in much the same manner. Articulations in the woodwind section are not essentially different from bowings in the string sections. The effect of the martelé or the grande detaché of the violins can be produced with reasonable accuracy by the clarinet players, and even the pizzicato can be imitated by a skillful oboist without too much loss of fidelity. All ordinary forms of legato playing can be treated with equal effectiveness by the string and woodwind sections. It would be quite ridiculous to assert that these two types of instruments can do all things equally well; but the entire process of teaching may be made somewhat more intelligible and the results of teaching definitely more unified and coherent by a recognition of the fact that all of the instruments speak a common language. The conductor will take a definite step toward the goal of better ensemble performance when he is able to develop the separate functions of the various sections while at the same time stressing their interdependence and their importance as parts of the larger structure. The families of wind instruments, too, have many points in common: the entire reed family has a basic similarity in construction and fingering as does also the brass family. It would be well to make charts showing fingerings common to all woodwinds, and similar charts for all the brasses. This would be an invaluable aid to the student who may be asked to double on some other instrument.

Correct breathing habits are essential to the building of a substantial technique on any wind instrument, and fundamentally this is the breathing technique of the new-born babe before anyone has a chance to tell him to "fill up his chest" and "draw in his waist." When a deep breath is drawn into the lungs only a limited amount of expansion is normally possible around those parts of the lungs which are protected by the side walls and the ribs. If an abnormally large breath be drawn in, the only possible direction of expansion is downward, or against the diaphragmatic muscle. This downward pressure will force the lower ribs and the waist-line to expand, and conversely, as the breath is exhaled the waist-line contracts. This is the natural process, but unfortunately, many singers and players of wind instruments have not formed the correct habits of breathing or have had a normally correct habit disturbed by the belief that some different system of breathing must be required in singing or in the playing of an instrument.

The most important consideration must always be that the breathing be free and relaxed according to the natural pattern, but that there be what the singers call "support," which may be roughly described as the feeling that the diaphragm is gently pushing the breath up and out of the lungs as it is needed. In contrast to this system is one of utter neglect of the breathing process, resulting in shallow breathing, an inadequate supply of breath, and insufficient control of the flow of the breath stream. There are as many different methods of teaching and developing the correct breathing habits as there are private voice and wind instrument studios; consequently, the conductor who wishes to acquire one of these "methods" will find a wide range of choice. The important matter is to see that the player understands the process and makes a fairly consistent effort to establish it correctly as a habit. Posture will have a very considerable effect upon the final results.

It is interesting to note in connection with the question of breathing and breath control that the players of the double reed instruments face a difficulty that is quite unusual — the difficulty of having too much breath. Because of the small aperture in the reed and the small amount of breath required to sustain the vibration of the reed, the player has no ready means of changing the air in his lungs at the normal rate. This retention of "dead" air and the resultant lack of oxygen explain the fact that the oboist always appears to be working harder than any other wind instrument player.

The function of the tongue is an important one in the playing of any wind instrument. In the case of the reeds, its task is to close the opening between the reed and the mouthpiece in preparation for the actual start of the tone. The release of the tongue permits the breath to flow through the instrument, causing the reed to vibrate. The tongue does not, however, stop the vibration of the reed by a similar action. The player should stop the flow of breath by diaphragmatic control — not by means of the tongue or the throat muscles. Hence the discard of the old "toot" or "tut" method of teaching the young and the substitution of the "too" or "tu" method. The sharpness of the attack will depend upon three factors — the placement of the tongue against the reed, the force and suddenness with which it is withdrawn, and the extent of the breath pressure released at the instant of attack. There is much more that might be said concerning the breath technique of the woodwind instruments, but this much will provide a basis for such conductors as may not have previously understood the fundamental principles.

Finger technique is chiefly a matter of maintaining proper coverage of holes and keys with a maximum of controlled relaxation and in such a manner as to obviate all unnecessary movement of the fingers. A straight line is the shortest distance between two points, and this can be either a short line or a long line. The player of a woodwind instrument who moves the finger an inch or more each time he presses a key will consume twice as much time and energy as the player who moves the finger one-half inch; speed and flexibility are the essential factors in developing an adequate finger technique. There is also the most important matter of coordinating the actions of tongue, breath, and fingers. Some woodwind players are unable to achieve the best results because of their failure to develop skill in manipulating combinations of fingers. For example, if a given note calls for the use of the second finger of the right hand and the first and second fingers of the left hand, the action of these fingers must be simultaneous; otherwise the result will not be a cleanly executed interval but a series of three separate and distinct intermediate tones.

The embouchure (literally "mouthing") has much to do with the quality and the quantity of the tone produced. In the case of the single- and double-reed instruments the first rule is that the mouthpiece be held firmly with the lips, in order that there be no leakage of air and that proper control can be exerted upon the reed. Too pinched or tight an embouchure will have the same effect upon the tone as would a mute upon the tone of a stringed instrument; consequently, it is important that the lips be placed quite far down on the mouthpiece or the reed. A full flow of air must be allowed to pass into the instrument and the reed must be allowed to vibrate freely, thus producing a resonant, bell-like tone. It is always easier to modify and refine a tone when the habit of producing one of a more vibrant character has been established. In the case of the flute and the piccolo, the lips of the player function in directing the air-stream toward the farther edge of the blow-hole; and the quality and pitch will be determined by the size of the aperture, the force of the air-stream, and the angle at which it is directed into the blow-hole.

In the minds of most student players and many professionals the term "instrumental technic," when applied to a wind instrument, means that general group of skills which includes breathing, tonguing, and fingering. Only a relatively small number of musicians would place the special skill of *keeping in tune* near the top of the list of basic requirements; yet this is by far the most important single consideration whenever two or more instrumentalists undertake to play together. Fundamentally, this skill is based upon the necessity of changing a tone from its natural or usual pitch, either in anticipation of or in adjustment to the tone of another instrument or voice. This slight upward or downward modification of the pitch requires an instantaneous change in the pitch of one instrument to bring it into perfect sympathy with another. Upon the acceptance of this principle and the ability of most of the members of an ensemble to put the principle into practice depends the attainment of perfect intonation, blend of tone, and balance of voices.

A helpful device in establishing a "feeling" for harmonic balance and blend (which must always be based upon absolutely true intonation) is that of playing as sustained chords any series of complicated harmonies which may be encountered in the rehearsal.

The only instruments which are incapable of this sort of pitch adjustment are the piano, organ, harp, bells, xylophone, and similar keyboard-type instruments; and it is interesting to note that none of them are regarded as fixed elements in the orchestra or the band. When one of these is used as a solo instrument it becomes the responsibility of all other players to adjust to the pitch standard established by this one. There is no such thing as a perfectly tuned musical instrument. The modern piano represents a compromise between the pitch relationships as we naturally hear them and the practical advantages of having an instrument which can be played in any key. Bach established this pattern of tuning with his *Equal-tempered Clavichord*, and all other instruments have been constructed in accordance as far as possible; but the human ear still tends to follow the natural pattern. The pitch-sensitive singer and the string player who is thoroughly schooled in quartet playing unconsciously follow the unequal scale with its definite pitch leanings toward natural resolutions. Examples of these pitch tendencies are the close half-step between the leading tone and the octave and the downward trend of the subdominant toward the mediant in the V_7 and I progression. An excellent test of one's sensitiveness to these exaggerations of certain intervals is found in the playing of the harmonic form of the minor scale. If the sixth is not sharply depressed and the seventh raised perceptibly after several careful repetitions at slow speed, one can be fairly certain of one of two things: either that the performer has a naturally poor sense of pitch relationship or that his native capacity for discrimination has been dulled by too much playing and too little listening. In both melodic and harmonic relationships the treatment of accidental sharps, flats, and cancels (i.e., pitch determinations not contained in the key signature) calls for special care in the matter of pitch adjustment. The correct melodic or harmonic character will usually be achieved by exaggerating the pitch direction suggested by the accidental. A flat will suggest an excessive depression of the pitch, a sharped tone should be raised a very liberal half-step, while the direction of modification of the cancel will depend upon whether it nullifies a sharp or a flat.

Even the most accurately constructed wind instruments fail to measure up to the tuning standard of a well-tuned piano. In the case of the woodwind instruments, this is due to the mechanical difficulty of controlling all of the factors which might influence the pitch relationships throughout the range of the instrument. In the case of the brass instruments, it is explained by the fact that the valve slides cannot be made to provide the correct added tube length in all of the possible valve combinations. The result in either case is a mixture of deliberate compromise and pure accident. However, acoustical engineers at band instrument factories are constantly striving to improve both the intonation and the tone quality of all band instruments and are the first to admit that the absolutely perfect instrument has not yet been built. The matter is not too important in any case since, if the instrument were perfectly in tune according to the piano standard, the player would still have to make such pitch adjustments as might be dictated by any leaning of natural intervals. It is a recognized fact that the best possible wind instrument can be played out of tune and that an instrument which is not too badly off-pitch can be made to sound in tune. This can be quickly and easily demonstrated by any competent player. The conclusion to be drawn from this is simply that each player must be impressed with the importance of making these slight pitch adjustments, and he must be taught the actual technique of pitch variation.

The answer to the inevitable question: Who determines the pitch? is fairly easy to supply. The rough tuning is done to a tuning bar, oboe, or clarinet; the usual chords and scales are employed as a further check; and the lead players in each section are admonished to cross-check their intonation in every possible way. Thus, within the orchestra or band, we have what amounts to a small woodwind ensemble and a small brass ensemble of different instruments, the players of which assume major responsibility for the maintenance of a standard pitch. Beyond this point the adjustments are made on the basis of the pitch standard of whichever instrument happens to be playing a solo part or the most prominent voice in a harmonic passage. If one solo instrument follows another, the second player adopts the pitch of the first. There are other variations of this system, but in practice the players usually know which voice to accept as the standard. The method might seem to suggest the probability of a constantly fluctuating pitch level, but this will not be the case if a reasonably fixed standard is established at the outset and if the section leaders accept the responsibility of maintaining this standard. The principal virtue of the pitch modification technique is that it tends toward breaking down the prevailing idea that all that is necessary, once the instruments are "tuned," is for the players to press certain keys, and blow, at the proper time.

The woodwind section of the orchestra or the band presents a great many problems for the conductor; but if these problems are solved with even a modicum of success, the results will be rich in satisfaction to both performers and listeners, for the woodwind instruments provide the color of any organization. The technical and the expressive possibilities of this group of instruments are practically unlimited, and they are capable of a flexibility matched only by the strings.

CHAPTER X

Brass Instruments

All that has been stated in the preceding chapter concerning the breathing technique, tongue action, embouchure, and pitch adjustment applies, with only slight modification, to the playing of the brass instruments. There is, however, this essential difference between the woodwind and the brass instruments, i.e., that whereas the source of the tone in the first instance is a bamboo reed (or the force of a split air-stream in the case of the flute), the vibrating media of the brass instruments are the lips of the players. This difference suggests the possibility that the player of the woodwind instrument is, generally speaking, more dependent upon his instrument, whereas the player of the brass instrument is more dependent upon himself, or at least upon his lips and his teeth. Various studies have been undertaken to discover whether there is actually any high degree of correlation between performance on brass instruments and lip musculature and evenness of teeth, but these investigations have provided no conclusive proof either for or against such relationship. In practice, several other factors seem to overbalance these two as determinators of success or failure.

The fact that the tone of the brass instrument is actually produced by the lips of the player, however, does raise the question of the comparative difficulty of the brass and the woodwind instruments and the relative length of time required for gaining an elementary playing technique. A prospective instrumentalist, upon examining superficially a clarinet and a cornet, will invariably choose the latter because he thinks that it will be the easier to play. The complicated mechanism of the clarinet suggests untold difficulties by comparison with the three valves of the cornet. Actually the cornet may be the more difficult to play for the following reasons: 1. the necessity of developing the lips so that they will vibrate evenly without tiring; 2. the fact that this lip control must be such as to make possible a differentiation between tones played with the same fingering but with different embouchure adjustments; 3. the lesser problem of mastering the various valve combinations. The apparent simplicity of the cornet technique probably accounts for the fact that many more players select brass instruments than woodwind instruments. If a reasonable balance between the two types is to be maintained, the students should be guided in their choice by the conductor or teacher.

Mastery of brass instrument technique is a long and difficult process. If it is properly approached, the initial period will be devoted almost exclusively to the practice of sustained tones within a very limited range and with moderate dynamic intensity. An entirely new function of the player's lips must be developed, and this cannot be forced any more than the muscle of an arm may be made strong by violent and exhausting exercise. Alternate periods of practice and rest will gradually build a lip capable of meeting the strenuous demands which will be made upon it in the course of normal playing requirements. Many brass instrument players are ruined in the first months of their training by a too-ambitious and unwise forcing of their development, and once the damage has been done it is difficult, if not impossible, to effect a remedy.

As has already been stated, the quality of tone produced by a string player or by a woodwind player depends quite largely upon purely mechanical factors inherent in the instrument. If the violin is a finely constructed instrument — made of good material, strung with highest quality strings, and properly adjusted in every respect — the tone will be reasonably satisfactory even though the bow be drawn by a relatively unskilled player. The same is true of a clarinet provided the player is advanced beyond the most elementary stage, but it is less true of the flute because of the fact that the vibration is more directly the result of the player's skill and training. This is not to suggest that the tone of any instrument will not improve with the ability of the player, but in the case of the brass instruments the tone simply does not exist until the lips of the player have been developed. In the strings and the woodwinds the tone is largely present in the instruments themselves, being produced in the one instance by a vibrating string and in the other by a vibrating reed.

The player of a brass instrument will probably not be able to produce a beautiful tone until he gains a correct conception of tone, and herein lies the advantage of his studying under an instructor who actually plays the instrument and plays it well. The same applies with equal force to every other instrument, but it is emphasized at this point because of the inadequacy of the brass tone heard in many school bands and orchestras. Whatever the instrument, tone quality is the most important single consideration because it is the material of which music is made. The listener is not in the least interested in the number of notes that can be played per minute; or how high, or how loudly, or even how softly the players can play, unless the tone be of pleasing quality. There is, of course, a definite place in musical expression for the use of a tone which is not beautiful *per se*, but this is the exception and not the rule. Since music covers the whole range of descriptive possibilities a harsh or raucous tone is perfectly legitimate if used in the right place for the right purpose, but the basic tone should be pleasing and esthetically satisfying. It must be one of the teacher's first responsibilities to establish proper standards in the matter of tone quality; and whether this is done through the use of recordings, actual demonstrations by competent performers on the various instruments, or by the trial and error method of glorifying the best tone produced within the group while decrying that which is faulty, the end will justify the means. This need is especially urgent with reference to the brass instruments in view of the deleterious influence of the marching band, the so-called "pep" band, and last but not least, some of the lesser radio dance bands.

In the preceding chapter a parallel was drawn between the technical processes underlying the production of vocal music and that of the wind instruments. This parallel is even more clearly defined between the human voice and the brass instruments, particularly as concerns the character of the music produced by these two media. While the brass instruments are capable of a wide variation of expression, ranging from the dignified and pompous ceremonial march to the insistent and penetrating blare of a Tschaikowsky symphony, they are at their best in the purely vocal idiom. The more boisterous forms of expression are much less exacting, and in such passages the shortcomings of the individual player are perhaps less subject to detection; but the real test of a player is his ability to execute a sustained, flowing melody well within the lower dynamic levels and with that consummate ease and flexibility which characterize the artist and the skilled executant. For every brass instrument player who can acquit himself in this commendable manner there are fifty who can thrill the less discerning audience with a brilliantly executed triple-tongue polka with variations. If real and lasting progress is to be made in the field of brass instrument performance, the standards of training and the goals of ultimate musical achievement must be re-defined.

Both numerically and dynamically the cornets lead the field of brass players in the public schools and also, it might be added, in the colleges and universities. In one of the larger institutions of higher learning the band organization of something less than two hundred players includes almost fifty cornetists. This situation is to be expected as long as the secondary schools continue to admit a disproportionate number of these instruments. For the ultimate protection of the players themselves definite restrictions should be placed upon the number of cornet players who may be accepted in the secondary school organizations, and those rejected should be urged to take up other instruments of which there is a shortage in college bands and orchestras.

The term cornet is used generically and includes the trumpet as well as an instrument known as a trumpet-cornet or cornet-trumpet. There should be a definite place for the extreme types of both the cornet and the trumpet, and also for the related fluegelhorn, but at the present time the band conductor is in very much of a quandary as to the possible uses he might make of these three kinds of instruments. Their tone qualities are quite distinct – that of the cornet representing a median, with the more brilliant and penetrating tone of the trumpet at one extreme and the more rich and flexible tone of the fluegelhorn at the other. The confusion in the mind of the conductor may be traced to the fact that the arrangements of concert band music make no recognizable distinction between these three instruments, the parts being doubled, overlapped, and interchanged without regard for their special characteristics. In the orchestra, of course, the trumpet is usually designated, and in the standard literature the parts are generally true to the character of the instrument. In many adaptations for school orchestra, on the other hand, a cornet would suit more nearly the nature of the melodies written for the instrument. The only apparent remedy for such errors in musical judgment is to rewrite the parts to suit the instruments which are available, but this is an arduous and exacting task, and many conductors will not consider the results worth the time and effort required. A suggested compromise for the band conductor is to have, in addition to the cornets and trumpets, at least one fluegelhorn to which may be assigned any parts which seem suited to the rich, appealing character of this little-used instrument.

The fluegelhorn, which achieves its deeper resonance of tone as a result of a larger bore and a more gradual bell flare, is a distinct addition to the cornet group in the band. It adds a fuller body of tone and tends to reduce to some extent the shrill and penetrating quality of the higher brasses. If its use actually does improve the tone quality of the cornet and trumpet section, is it not reasonable to expect that a like improvement might be effected throughout the rest of the brass section by the inclusion of more instruments of this type? The problematical angle of the question is stressed because too few bands have been able to assemble a full complement of the larger bore instruments to prove the contention. In recent years the trend has been toward the relatively smaller bore and the bell-front type of instrument, even to the basses; and while this has contributed to the brilliance of the band, it has not improved either the tone quality or the blend of the brass section. Brilliance and carrying power may be desirable on the march, but these qualities are not of supreme importance in the concert hall. If the symphonic band is ever to achieve distinction as a musical organization, it must be equipped with a radically different type of brass instrument than those now in common use. Along with the liberal use of fluegelhorns, with cornets and no more than two trumpets, there should be larger-bore and larger-bell euphoniums, baritones, trombones, and basses, the upright model basses being preferred to the bell-front sousa-phone type. To complete the range of the brass instruments the E-flat bass should be added, conditional upon a complete revision of the parts as now written for the basses.

In performance, the brass sections of both band and orchestra (and this applies as well to the woodwind sections) may be criti-cized for their failure to achieve a real sostenuto. No fault is more common than this, and none so certain to destroy the effectiveness of an ensemble. Due no doubt to the circumstance that one must breathe to live, the players of wind instruments invariably seem to fall into the habit of too-frequent breath-taking which breaks even the shortest phrases and converts what should be flowing melodies and beautiful sustained harmonies into a series of meaningless musical fragments. In slow time the usual habit of most amateurs is to breathe at the end of every second measure, and the absolute limit of endurance is usually four measures! There are, of course, some forms which can be broken in this manner without loss of musical effect-iveness, but when this system of breathing becomes so firmly estab-lished that the players must always breathe at these points, the inter-pretation is sure to suffer. More often than not, the wind parts, and especially the brass parts, can be made much more effective if the phrase ends are bridged over without any perceptible break for breath. This is accomplished in one of two ways, either by postpon-ing the taking of breath beyond the phrase to a convenient break in a subsequent measure or by breathing in relays within each section. This latter practice — "staggering" the taking of breath — is in com-mon usage in the best of the present day choruses, and it has proved to be a highly effective device in the development of a fine sostenuto in the band.

Other common faults which spring from the same cause — short-ness of breath due to poor breathing habits — are what might be termed the "unconscious decrescendo" and the habit of shortening single notes or phrases which are followed by rests. For example, a dotted half-note in slow four-quarter time will be released by the careless amateur at the beginning of the third count instead of at the end of the third or the start of the fourth count. Ordinarily there should be little or no dynamic change in a closing note or chord unless, of course, a change is definitely specified. The release of a fortissimo tone, as in a chord for full band or orchestra, should not end with that explosive quality so often heard in the performance of amateur groups. This is a rather cheap device, suggestive of cymbal crashes and vaudeville orchestras, and its use in serious music should be avoided. Another fairly common fault, especially among brass players, is the disregard of a crescendo indicated at the end of one phrase and leading into a climactic chord at the beginning of the next. Many players, in order to be prepared to bring in the climactic chord with maximum force, will take a breath just as they are sup-posed to be supplying the crescendo! These are but a few of the most common failures in breath technique. Others will be observed by the conductor who listens with a critical ear, but most of them may be quickly and easily remedied.

The method of attack employed by most brass instrument play-ers is essentially the same as has already been described in connec-tion with the reed instruments except that instead of the tip of the tongue being placed against the reed in preparation for the start of the tone, the tip of the tongue is placed either against the upper teeth or against the roof of the mouth just back of the teeth, depending upon the force of attack desired. The sudden withdrawal of the tongue permits the air-stream to project itself against the lips and set up the vibration which produces the tone. No attempt is made to define the technique of tonguing in exact terms because there are so many widely different methods in use and the proponent of each method is sure that his is the one and only approach. At one extreme we have the school which favors the venerable "spitting technique" of attack. This is based upon the idea that the position and action of the cheeks, lips, tongue, and breath in starting the tone are ex-actly the same as those employed in the action of spitting a hair or a thread from the lips. With this method the tip of the tongue is placed between the lips and is then withdrawn suddenly. While this technique might be used for very special effects it is generally frowned upon as a standard practice by the best teachers.

If the brasses have lacked some of the flexibility of the other in-struments, this may be explained, in part at least, by the inability of brass instrument players to vary their attack. The same hard, rigid technique is employed by the large majority of brass players whether the tune be one of a brilliantly martial character or the merest breath of tone in support of a light woodwind or string solo passage. Any conductor or teacher who has attempted to coax from his brass sec-tion a really fine pianissimo attack will appreciate the magnitude of the problem. The usual brass attack has the character of the "pre-pared," or staccato attack which was described in connection with the discussion of string problems. Only a relatively small number of professional players seem to possess the ability to imitate the "float-ing" attack which is produced on the stringed instruments by brush-ing the string ever so lightly with the bow. Many brass instrument players will claim that this is not possible on their instruments, but it has been demonstrated that it can be done by any player who is will-ing to adapt his technique to a new set of requirements. In this con-nection it must be remembered that the chief function of the brass instruments in the symphony orchestra has been to supply the heavy chordal structure and to punctuate the musical prose of the string body. In the modern symphonic band, on the other hand, the brasses serve quite a different purpose. Here they become, on occasion, the principal melodic element and as such they must possess a very wide range of expressive capacity. There is no place for a hard and explosive attack in the treatment of a beautifully liquid melodic passage, and the sooner the brass experts discover a method of eliminating this disturbing element, the sooner will the brass instruments be accepted as full-fledged members of the artistic fellowship. A suggested approach, applicable to the woodwinds as well as to the brasses, is to eliminate the tongue action entirely for the very soft attack. This method of starting the tone, literally "on the breath," demands the most sensitive adjustment and control of the lips in order that the initial vibration may be started without dependence upon a sudden release of breath pressure.

Since all tone produced upon a brass instrument arises from the vibration of the player's lips, it has been discovered that one of the very best technical approaches is that of "lip-buzzing." To buzz the lips in a fair approximation of ordinary playing procedure will involve attention to both correct breathing habits and embouchure adjustment. The evenness with which the player can sustain any given buzz-tone, and the extent of the pitch range, will largely determine his capacity to control the actual tone on the instrument. Experimentation and practice in lip-buzzing, with and without the mouthpiece of the instrument, will aid greatly in the development of flexibility and control.

Major emphasis has been given to such elements as tone quality, flexibility of manipulation, attack, and release because these are the matters most commonly neglected by amateur brass players and because upon their mastery must depend the attainment of true artistry. This does not imply, however, that the development of power and endurance is not equally important for general playing purposes. The brass instruments provide the heroic quality in the ensemble, and there are times when every player must be able to produce a tone of the greatest intensity. In sustained fortissimo passages a great physical strain is placed upon the brass player, and his training and preparation must be such as to fit him for this task without injury to his lips or undue stress upon his breathing mechanism. The approach to this phase of his playing technique should be gradual and should be marked by the exercise of extreme caution. The practice of sustained tones in the higher dynamic levels and throughout the normal playing range of the instrument will constitute the principal means of developing this essential technical skill. The playing of evenly-sustained tones should be supplemented by practice of the crescendo and the decrescendo.

The brass instruments will probably require less attention in matters of adjustment and repair than any of the others. Being solidly constructed of durable metals and not requiring any dismantling for storage (except in the case of the trombone and certain others), there is little reason for the adjustment being disturbed. With reasonable care, chiefly in cleaning and oiling, a brass instrument should give excellent service for many years. The French horn, constructed of a softer material and having the more complicated rotary valve mechanism, is usually the first of the brasses to be sent to the repair shop. For the most part, however, the conductor will experience little difficulty in keeping his brass instruments in acceptable playing condition.

No organization is better than its brasses, and no brass section is better than its weakest member. Many an otherwise ordinary orchestra or band has been made to appear a much better organization than it really was because of the harmonic clarity and the balance of its brass group and because the details of execution within this section had been subjected to careful analysis by the conductor and painstaking practice by the various players.

CHAPTER XI

Percussion Instruments

The technical and artistic attainments which have marked the progress of school orchestras and bands in recent years are nowhere reflected with greater fidelity than in the percussion sections of these organizations. Within comparatively recent times all drummers, excepting a few of the finest professionals, were self-taught. A good sense of rhythm was deemed a sufficient prerequisite for admission to the percussion section of the band or the orchestra, and once admitted, the player was guided chiefly by intuition and his ability to bluff his way through the more complicated rhythmic labyrinths. The percussion personnel and equipment of even some of the better school organizations of the early days consisted of one player, a bass drum with attached cymbal and foot pedal, a snare drum, and a few odds and ends of extra equipment. Fortunately these days are past in all but the most backward of school situations.

The percussion section of the better modern orchestra or band is well-manned and well-equipped. The larger groups usually include from three to six players and these players are provided with every conceivable type of percussion instrument. In some instances the percussion section has grown too large for the good of the organization of which it is a part, and very frequently it has been developed to the point of being the main attraction. Over-emphasis of this sort is not in the least unusual when new instruments or new uses of old instruments are in the process of development. It was true of the saxophone, the metal clarinet, the small bore trumpet, pre-orchestra and pre-band instruments, and baton twirling. The teacher or conductor who is looking for a new toy – a device with which to impress his constituency – will be quick to adopt and exploit any novel idea. This trend has been encouraged in the field of the percussion instruments by the popularity of the drum corps and the competitive spirit between schools. One of the surest tests of the conductor's musicianship is to be found in his concept of the percussion section. If he develops the section in terms of his actual requirements, in regard to both personnel and equipment, and if he utilizes the section as a functional and unobtrusive part of the organization, he is probably a musician. If, on the other hand, the percussion section is over-manned and over-equipped and if the players have developed an ostentatious style in their playing, the conductor is probably more a showman than he is a musician.

The percussion equipment required for a particular performance will always be determined by an analysis of the scores and parts of the compositions to be played. This will also govern the number of players to be used. With all due consideration of the personal and psychological advantages of including all regular members of an organization in its public appearances, there seems little to justify the common practice of having the complete personnel and percussion equipment on the platform for a performance which, for example, might call for only one player and a pair of tympani. For rehearsals, when it is not known in advance which numbers are to be played, it is advisable to have the full equipment and all percussion players available.

The minimum equipment for orchestra or band will include one pair of tympani, a bass drum, one concert snare drum, a pair of cymbals, and perhaps a triangle and a set of orchestra bells. Beyond this there is practically no limit to the amount of percussion equipment which might be required at one time or another, depending upon the size of the organization and the type of music which it plays. An extra pair of tympani will frequently be needed, as will the xylophone or marimba, tubular chimes, gong, temple blocks, special cymbals, wood-blocks, sand-blocks, castanets, tambourines, sleigh-bells, whistles, and the like. The number of players required will depend upon their versatility and the extent to which the different percussion parts can be consolidated. Where five or six different instruments are to be played simultaneously, this number of players must be available.

The arrangement or disposition of the percussion instruments within the orchestra or band set-up will also depend to some extent upon the number and versatility of the players. If one player is to handle several instruments, these instruments must be so placed that they are within easy reach of this player. For example, it is fairly customary in the larger bands to place the tympani on one side at the rear and all other percussion instruments in a corresponding position on the other side. If, however, the tympani player happens to be the only percussionist capable of playing the bell parts, it is obvious that the bells must be placed near the tympani. No two organizations will present exactly the same problem with reference to this matter of the placement of equipment. From the standpoint of the conductor, versatility is the most desirable quality in a percussionist, and this implies competence in each of the various fields of performance. A player who can play only one of the percussion instruments is of little value to an organization, and there is a strong probability that his playing of the single instrument would be vastly improved by some experience upon additional instruments within the section. Too much specialization by the percussionist works something of a hardship upon the conductor by making it necessary for him to adhere to a rigid system of playing assignments, and it may also prevent a player's gaining admission to a musical organization. If the conductor is faced with a choice between two individuals, one a tympanist only and the other a player who can handle tympani and snare or bass drums with about equal facility, he will almost certainly select the latter player. The fact that the college and university bands and orchestras have experienced some difficulty in recent years in finding truly versatile percussionists would seem to indicate that the high school conductors have failed to stress the importance of this matter. From an educational point of view the practice of requiring percussionists to work all of the different instruments can be justified. A still better device would be to encourage players of other band and orchestral instruments to gain some experience upon the rhythmic instruments.

The average conductor, being preoccupied with a great many details of organization, frequently neglects to make specific assignments of parts for the percussionists. As a result, essentials parts will often be overlooked or deliberately omitted by the players. It is the old problem of "what is every one's business is no one's business," and the organization suffers the loss, either through the absence of essential tonal effects or through confusion and waste of time in rehearsal. The obvious remedy is for the conductor to appoint a section leader who is responsible for analyzing all of the percussion parts and apportioning them to the various players in advance of the rehearsal. Naturally this section leader must be familiar with all of the percussion instruments, he should be capable of commanding the support of the other players, and he must work closely with the conductor in the solution of any problems which might arise.

The personal, intellectual, and musical qualifications of the drummer should be at least the equal of those demanded of any other instrumentalist. Because of the fact that the drummer must handle valuable equipment which is often the property of the school or other members of the section, he must be dependable in material matters. Since the part he plays is usually an independent part, he must be painstaking and accurate in his approach to technical and rhythmic problems. He must possess a discriminating judgment as to the relationship between the part he plays and the work of the entire ensemble. His sense of rhythm must be even more subtle and dependable than of most other players. He must understand time values with a certainty exceeded only by that of the conductor. He must possess an extremely high muscular coordination. He must be alert, mentally and physically. And finally, he must have a keen appreciation of musical values in order that his playing of the percussion parts be fully in sympathy with the melodic line, especially as concerns tempo variations and dynamic balance. Perhaps these requirements are too exacting. Possibly they are such as might be set forth for the concertmaster, or even the conductor; but in actual practice no member of a musical organization is of greater importance than the percussionist. He can add immeasurably to the musical effectiveness of the group or he can be a disturbing element in an otherwise excellent organization. The technically competent and artistic percussionist will always be in demand.

Excellent first steps toward developing the technical side of the art of drumming have been the inclusion of the drum solo event in the music contests and the formation of the National Association of Rudimental Drummers. To sit through several hours of a drum solo contest session is a trying experience, but the stimulation of interest in good drumming has justified the inclusion of this event in the contest program. However, its blessings have been definitely of the mixed variety. Performance upon any instrument must represent a balance between technique and expression, and unless this balance is maintained throughout the training period the result will be unsatisfactory on one side or the other. A performance which is rich in expressive possibilities without sufficient technical foundation is al-

ways a disappointment, but one which is based upon technical proficiency to the exclusion of musical ideas is worse than bad — it is
hopeless. This has been the principal achievement of those who have
stressed rudimental drumming without placing a parallel emphasis
upon purely musical considerations. Skill in the execution of flams,
paradiddles, and flamacues on a snare drum may be of the utmost
importance, but so also is the ability to execute a pianissimo roll and
to follow a subtle ritardando. These and hundreds of other details
of practical playing technique are disregarded in the rudimental
regimen as practiced by the great majority of student drummers.
Furthermore, the emphasis has been placed entirely upon snare
drumming without any attention having been given to tympani, bells,
cymbals, and the smaller traps which are of equal importance in actual
performance.

Technical facility, even if it be equally distributed throughout
the percussion section, still remains only one factor of several which
are important to the development of a well-rounded battery. Attention to the counting of rests is probably the one point at which
amateur drummers fail most frequently. This may be traced to
several factors, including natural carelessness, the delegation of responsibility to others in the section, the lack of a dependable method
of counting extended rest periods, and lack of confidence in one's
accuracy of counting. The substitution of instinct and guesswork
for practiced efficiency in counting will never produce the desired
results. One of the most effective means of checking the counting
habits of the percussionists is to turn the spotlight of publicity upon
their work by asking the entire section to play alone, without either
moral or actual support from the remainder of the orchestra or band.
If this process involves the counting of a considerable number of
measures of rest, the benefits of the device will be entirely lost by
skipping over these periods. The conductor should insist that they
be counted out meticulously and subsequent entrances brought in
with accuracy and assurance. If this cannot be done without supporting melody and harmony, it will prove rather conclusively that
the percussion players are in the habit of depending too largely upon
ensemble instinct and pure luck. An occasional percussion section
rehearsal will help greatly to develop unity within the group. In
connection with such rehearsals it is an excellent practice to have
all members of the section count their rest measures aloud. Even a

limited amount of practice along this line — treating the counting as a game or a stunt — will help to develop accuracy and dependability.

The conductor who is sensitive to the more subtle musical values in other sections of his orchestra or band will do well to expect and demand the same response from his drummers. Some of the very finest artists among the professional symphony players are percussionists, and their student counterparts may be found in high school and college organizations in which the conductors have emphasized the importance of perfect ensemble and the interdependence of the sections. Where the artistic ideal has been held high and where no single section has been permitted to fall below an acceptable standard, the percussion players will be among the most enthusiastic disciples of good music. A drummer usually tires of ordinary routine work in an organization which permits indiscriminate faking, and if given an opportunity to do something which he regards as exacting and artistic, he will frequently respond with even more interest than many of those who enjoy the advantage of playing melodic or harmonic parts. Once the percussionist appreciates his real importance in the ensemble, he will usually devote himself to the task of measuring up to his responsibilities.

Real finesse in drumming depends, of course, upon basic skills and upon a thorough knowledge of time problems. Beyond this it is important that the percussion player have a general understanding of such musical terms as might appear in the parts, for it must be remembered, the drum score will not contain any melodic material which might suggest the proper changes of tempo. Such terms as allegro, piu mosso, subito, and allargando may be the drummer's only guides, whereas the violinist has the advantage of following a melodic line which reflects, in large measure, the spirit and movement of the composition.

If the task of playing the correct rhythmic patterns, and playing them with the rest of the ensemble, may be accepted as the first and most important responsibility of the percussionist, then certainly the next most exacting requirement has to do with the question of dynamic treatment. It is most difficult for the drummer himself to gauge the dynamic force of his playing with any degree of accuracy. He is so near to his own instrument and to other percussion instruments that he cannot judge the force of his strokes with the same accuracy as can the conductor or the listener in the audience. To still further complicate his problem the drummer is usually placed in the far corner of the orchestra or band and behind the other instruments where it is difficult for him to hear exactly what goes on within the general ensemble. A solid wall immediately back of the percussion section does not help matters in the least. Many conductors fail to appreciate the full force of these handicaps under which the percussionists work, and as a result, they may not always be as helpful and considerate as might be desired. The members of the organization should appreciate the nature of this problem; and it should be understood by all that it is the conductor's function to help the percussionists check their own treatment of dynamics.

In this connection it must be stated that the great majority of drummers play with far too much force. Conductors often become immune to the constant "thumping" of the drums in rehearsal, and by imperceptible degrees this percussive effect increases to the point at which it is definitely obnoxious to any person not hardened to it by constant proximity. For many sensitive musicians this overplaying in the percussion section is almost painful, and it may explain the skepticism with which many persons regard the musical efforts of amateur groups in which a heavy treatment of the percussion parts seems to be one of the chief characteristics. Bands are usually the worst offenders in this regard.

Many authorities have spoken with emphasis upon this matter of unrestricted "pounding" on the part of the percussionists. One leading university band conductor, himself a drummer of recognized ability, expressed his view of the matter rather academically, but none the less effectively, when he said: "Not one bass drum stroke in fifty should impinge itself upon the consciousness of the listener." He might better have made it not one in five hundred strokes, but the implication is quite clear that the only bass drum strokes which should actually be heard are those intended to serve a special dramatic or descriptive purpose. Another well-known band conductor stated essentially the same thought when he asserted that "the bass drum should be felt, not heard!" These statements have been made with reference to the bass drum, but they apply with equal force to all of the percussion instruments. The snare drums and cymbals can offend in the same manner, and even the bell player usually strikes the bars with full force, not realizing that a light stroke with a small steel beater will be heard more easily and with much greater pleasure.

Such matters as the fundamental techniques of drumming and the care and conditioning of the percussion instruments may be safely left to the authors of drum instruction books and to the manufacturers of drum equipment who have been so very liberal in supplying brochures on all manner of problems relating to the percussion field. First-class instruments should require only a minimum amount of repair and reconditioning, provided proper care is exercised in keeping the tension of the heads even and in cleaning and oiling screws and other friction points. Temperature and humidity control are important factors in the preservation of drum heads and in maintaining their flexibility and resonance.

Every conductor has been faced, at one time or another, with the unsolved problem of drum notation. This is probably but another evidence of the careless attitude toward drumming and drummers held by the conductors, composers, arrangers, and publishers of an earlier day. It may have been assumed that the drummer would be more or less of an improviser in any case, and consequently no special effort was made to provide him with a readable part. In general, this has not been true of the standard orchestral material, although even in this field one occasionally finds parts which cannot be translated with any certainty that they represent the ideas of the composer. For example, what distinction did Dvorak have in mind when he scored this passage for tympani?

Allegro molto

When Tschaikowsky indicated a note for cymbal, what *kind* of a cymbal stroke did he have in mind — the clash of two cymbals together (large or small?) or a suspended cymbal struck with a beater, and if the latter, what kind of a beater? There are dozens of different effects which can be produced in different ways, and the ultimate decision rests entirely with the conductor. In every other field of instrumental writing the conductor is able to interpret the score with a reasonable consistency and a fair degree of fidelity to the composer's wishes, but this is not always true of the percussion parts.

The chief offenders in this vital matter have not been the recognized masters of symphonic literature but the composers, arrangers, and publishers of music especially designed for the use of school, amateur, and commercial instrumental organizations. In these editions the snare drum part constitutes a reasonably accurate guide, but the bass drum and cymbal parts leave much to the imagination and inventive genius of the performer. There is usually no way of knowing whether the bass drum is to be played with or without the cymbal; and when a cymbal crash is indicated, there still exists the uncertainty already referred to regarding the manner in which it should be executed. The percussion parts are, in general, much too ponderous, and they are often lacking in variety, interest, and conformity with the character of the composition. In numbers containing both tympani and bass drum parts to be played simultaneously, the former is usually the correct part and should stand alone. For the convenience of groups which do not have tympani, a substitute bass drum part has been added. Some publishers have indicated that this part is to be used only in the absence of the tympani, but others have overlooked this important detail with the result that all of the heavy percussion instruments participate. This combination of the tuned tympani with the drums, which have indefinite pitches, is extremely unsatisfactory and should be avoided except for very special effects.

The percussion parts in a transcription of a work composed originally for orchestra should be checked against the orchestral score. It is usually best to retain the original percussion parts to whatever degree is consistent with other features of the transcription. Occasionally one finds a transcription in which new percussion instruments have been added without loss of the original coloring, and in a few instances the effectiveness of a composition has been enhanced by the use of a part which is quite different from the original. In many more cases, however, the arrangers have weakened rather than strengthened standard works through the introduction of new and inappropriate percussion tone. One example of this is the cymbal crash in a band transcription of one of the Bach chorales! Good taste and fidelity to the intent of the composer or the medium for which the composition was originally written should be the guiding principle in all transcription, but this principle must be applied with particular care in the treatment of the percussion parts.

The contribution which the percussion instruments make to the modern concert band and to the orchestra cannot be valued too highly from an artistic point of view. As purely rhythmic background material, as dramatic or descriptive elements, as the chief source of nationalistic coloring in the ensemble fabric, and as a contributing factor in the building of powerful tonal climaxes the percussion instruments have earned a place of importance in the orchestra and in the band. Their function cannot be fulfilled by any other instrument or any combination of instruments. If the percussion instruments have been neglected in the past, it is only because composers, conductors, and arrangers have not recognized their importance in the instrumental ensemble and have not accorded them the same opportunities and encouragement that have been the lot of the string, woodwind, and brass instruments.

CHAPTER XII

Technical Instruction and Drill

The term "technic," when used with reference to performance upon a musical instrument, is usually understood to apply to those purely physical or mechanical operations involved in the manipulation of the instrument. This connotation is most commonly accepted by those who possess only a superficial knowledge of music and the processes involved in its production. Actually it is sometimes difficult to draw a fine line of distinction between the various elements in performance, and to say that certain of these elements are essentially technical and that others are non-technical.

The performance of the Strauss *Perpetual Motion* might pass as a purely technical feat, requiring only a minimum of interpretative ability, whereas the *Aria* from Bach's *Suite No. 3 in D Major* (best known in its transcribed form for violin as the *Air on the G String*) would impress most listeners as a composition demanding special ability in the matter of interpretation. It is true that these two compositions are of vastly different types, but it can hardly be said that one is any less exacting than the other in either technic or interpretation. Each calls for a special kind of skill, and the point at which this skill ceases to be technical and becomes interpretative the performers themselves would hardly be able to determine.

If the term may be used in its broader sense, there are many kinds of technique inherent in any musical performance. In addition to the technique of manipulating bows, fingers, and keys, there is the technique of tone production, the technique of dynamic control, and even the technique of interpretation. These latter techniques, which have to do mainly with expression, have too often been regarded as God-given gifts and not mechanical processes of a sort to be analyzed, taught, and practiced. While it is true that some players seem to choose instinctively the mechanical means which will produce the best results in interpretation, this does not prove conclusively that those who do not possess the gift of expression may not acquire it. Many musicians have been handicapped at the outset by having a poor rhythmic sense or limited muscular coordination, but thousands of such individuals have succeeded in mastering the complexities of time and movement and have become skilled executants. Is there any valid reason to suppose that the same results may not be achieved in the realm of expression or interpretation? The field of music education needs, more than anything else, teachers who are themselves highly sensitive to musical values, who know how to translate the essential elements of expression into terms which can be understood by students, and who believe that interpretation *can be taught*.

The psychological and physiological processes involved in performances upon a musical instrument are essentially the same whether the emphasis is placed upon the technical or upon the interpretative elements. There can be no properly directed manipulation of the instrument without processes of thought and feeling, and there can be no expression of ideas or emotions without appropriate muscular action. Hence it must be recognized that the entire process of playing and interpreting is based upon an interdependence of all of the mental, emotional, and physical phenomena. Any attempt to differentiate between the various phases of performance must, of necessity, be regarded as essentially artificial and must be adopted only for purposes of convenience.

Conductors of orchestras and bands have encountered a type of difficulty which seems to fall quite naturally into the general category of technique in its commonly accepted sense. This problem might be described more accurately as one of coordination. Fundamentally, it rests upon the difficulty of obtaining from a number of different players exactly the same tempo, the same rhythmic response, the same dynamic force, the same degree of retard or acceleration, and strict uniformity of attack and release. In a sense, these are technical problems. Certainly their solution rests upon a highly mechanical process involving the analysis of time values, emphasis upon grouping and accenting, and a strict adherence to the broader metrical outlines of the composition under preparation. For the most part, these problems are not such that they can be solved by individual study or practice. They are essentially related to ensemble performance, and the best solution for them is found in the general rehearsal. Although a large part of every rehearsal is devoted to the correction of these slight, but none the less serious flaws in reading or execution, this special phase of orchestral and band training has not been generally recognized as a distinct element. For want of a better term it might be referred to as the "technique of coordination."

The exact nature of this problem of mechanical coordination might be more fully appreciated if the reader could imagine an orchestra or a band composed entirely of players who had received all of their training in private studios under different teachers and who had never been members of any sort of instrumental ensemble. All of these players might have been well-taught; but the fact that they had been taught by diverse methods and that rhythmically, dynamically, and technically each player had been "a law unto himself" would lead to no end of difficulty in the first ensemble rehearsal. Music is so flexible a medium of expression that no two players, working independently, would be likely to follow exactly the same technical and interpretative pattern. The printed notes and symbols constitute only a rough guide to what actually happens in performance. It is within this area of variability that the individual players draw apart and thus disturb the ensemble. There must be a common understanding of detail — a unified feeling for the treatment of the variables — which can be developed only in the rehearsal.

Another factor which serves to emphasize the need for ensemble technical training or drill on the mechanical details of performance is the wide difference which exists between the technical and musical "idiom" of the orchestra or the band and that employed in most of the usual instructional material. Preparatory methods, études, and technical studies may completely cover the mechanics of violin playing, for example; but nowhere in this wealth of material is to be found the identical playing idiom which the violinist encounters in the orchestra. A violin étude is usually designed for a specific technical purpose, and this problem will be stressed throughout the work; but in the orchestra the violinist will discover a great variety of problems in close juxtaposition and interspersed with rest periods, sustained tones, and many more musical terms and dynamic markings than are usually found in the solo or training material. Upon first entering the orchestra the studio-taught violinist will face the task of learning a new dialect, if not a new language, and the same will apply to all other members of the orchestra or the band. The mastery of the new dialect is most quickly and efficiently achieved through a recognition by both the conductor and the player of the fundamental importance of the technique of coordination.

In recent years a number of unison studies for both orchestra and band have been published. These have served a most useful purpose in bridging the gap between individual and ensemble performance. Their principal weakness is that they stress only the more obvious technical problems such as scales in various forms, interval skips, common rhythmic patterns, and articulation or bowing. However, the use of such unison studies as may be available is strongly recommended, and it is suggested that the conductor incorporate into these exercises as much flexibility as possible in tempo and dynamics in order to avoid that metronomic and tonal rigidity which characterizes so many amateur performances.

The more exacting and infinitely more important process of working out the technical difficulties which are to be found in any worthwhile educational material must be based upon the conductor's skill in diagnosis. Like an experienced medical practioner he must first of all know the diseases and their symptoms. Having once isolated the source of the trouble, he suggests the remedy which he believes will cure the patient. Sometimes the doctor makes a wrong diagnosis, and very frequently the medicine prescribed does not prove effective in a particular case. Carrying the parallel to its logical conclusion, the patient sometimes grows worse instead of better, and when all attempts to find a cure have failed, the patient may die.

The musical physician makes his preliminary examination of the score (complete score, if procurable), and this examination is supplemented by more exhaustive and conclusive tests in the laboratory of the rehearsal. As a result of these later tests he may alter his findings and follow quite a different procedure than was first anticipated. If the first remedy to be applied does not prove effective, he may try another. Possibly it will be a combination of the two methods which will bring the desired results.

To set forth anything like a complete listing of the physical, or structural weaknesses which may be found in ensemble performance would be a task far beyond the scope of this work. The field of musical literature is too extensive and the number and variety of specific problems are far too great to permit an analysis sufficiently detailed to cover even the principal types of technical difficulties. Symphony orchestra conductors who have spent their entire lives in the study of scores still find new and interesting problems in works which they have conducted repeatedly, not to mention the even more complicated patterns which are being utilized by modern composers. Hence the few examples which will be included here must be regarded as only suggestive of the more common types of ensemble technical difficulties. If the method of analysis and the approach to a solution serve in any measure to establish a pattern for general use, the purpose of the study will have been fulfilled.

A somewhat elementary type of difficulty may be described as the "melody and accompaniment" pattern. The following example, presented in reduced score form, will illustrate this problem:

CAPRICCIO IN A – HAYDN (Orchestra)

(Woodwind and brass instruments follow the same basic patterns.)
Copyright by Theodore Presser Co., Philadelphia
Reprinted by permission

In a passage of this type the tendency is always to concentrate upon the melody and to neglect the accompaniment, with the result that the harmonic understructure lacks clarity. If the chord sequences are the least bit unusual or if special difficulties in fingering or reading are involved, the accompaniment may be definitely out of tune. Because of the fact that the chordal notes are short, there is little opportunity to listen carefully for the pitch relationships or to make adjustments which could be made if the tones were sustained. In aggravated cases the accompaniment is so indefinite in the matter of pitch that the effect is one of a series of characterless noises.

The procedure to be followed here is to have the passage played in very slow tempo, each tone being sustained to its full value. This will help to establish the tonality and the key or finger relationships. By gradually increasing the speed and shortening the notes, the accompaniment can be brought out with clarity of both harmony and rhythm. In all such passages the accompanying chords should be played somewhat more lightly than the solo voices.

Another common mechanical problem is presented in what might be termed "alternating passage work"—the assignment of parts of a continuous melody to different sections. An example of this is found in the same *Capriccio* by Haydn. It is as follows:

CAPRICCIO IN A – HAYDN (Orchestra)

The difficulties encountered in passages of this sort are chiefly those of maintaining an exact tempo and even distribution of time within the measure and of carrying the same volume of tone, or penetrating power, throughout the passage. It will be observed that the melody and the pitch are identical in each of the three statements, and consequently the three may be played in unison as the first step in securing a uniform speed. Various sequences may then be employed — bassoon and clarinet alternating, then bassoon and oboe, etc. — until the entrances and speeds are thoroughly coordinated. The technical fault in all such cases is apt to be that the players breathe and prepare the embouchure for the entrance too late. By anticipating his entrance each player will come in smoothly.

A somewhat similar problem is that which occurs in the well-known *Menuet* for strings by Bolzoni. Here there are no rests, but the essential melodic material may become lost in the adjacent accompanying parts. The excerpt is as follows:

"MINUETTO" – BOLZONI (For strings)

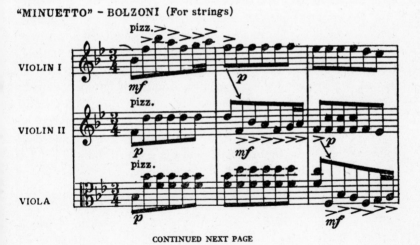

CONTINUED NEXT PAGE

(The cello and bass parts provide a simple tonic dominant accompaniment.)
Copyright by Theodore Presser Co., Philadelphia
Reprinted by permission

The first problem in this passage is to bring out the seven melodic notes as they occur in the three parts in order. This would appear to be an extremely easy task for the players, but in practice they seem unable to stress the notes which are important and then drop back into an accompanying character. As in the previous example, the three melodic figures may be played in unison as a means of impressing the melody upon the players' minds and of establishing a unified tempo. The next step might be to have only the melodies played, but in their regular sequence. Another helpful device is to ask the students to play only the accompaniment parts. Still another "teaching device" which challenges the attention of the players and secures the desired effect is to ask them to omit the single note which follows the melodic figure. In the end the essential thing is to have the melody stand out above all of the other material in clear, sharp contrast.

In ensemble literature one can find many examples of the difficulty which might be termed a "conflicting rhythm" problem, in which various closely related, but different, rhythmic patterns are used simultaneously or in close enough juxtaposition to cause some confusion for both the player and the listener. The following passage will illustrate:

OVERTURE "IN SPRINGTIME" – GOLDMARK (Band)

(These basic parts are duplicated in rhythm by other woodwind parts.)
"In Springtime" used by permission of the publishers,
C. L. Barnhouse Co., Oskaloosa, Iowa

There is no ready-made device for the solution of this problem. It exists as a problem only because of the possibility that immature players will lack sufficient independence to carry their own parts with convincing certainty. A suggestion by the conductor that care be exercised in the treatment of both the rhythm and the articulation should be sufficient to insure the desired results, but if this fails the only immediate remedy is to have each of the three conflicting parts — legato triplets, staccato duplets, dotted eighth and sixteenth pattern — played independently or with the pizzicato bass part for support. The characteristic feature of each pattern should be exaggerated, and any tendency on the part of the oboe or the third clarinet players to play a triplet accentuation should be corrected.

The excerpts from standard scores which appear in this chapter and elsewhere are intended primarily to illustrate specific problems in the teaching of orchestras and bands, but they may also serve an important secondary purpose. In a very real sense, they may be regarded as aptitude tests for the conductor — a sort of self-administered examination to determine whether or not he possesses a real interest in the mechanical aspects of instrumental writing. If his interest lies only in conducting superficial works which involve no complexities of rhythm, phrasing, dynamics, and accentuation, he will probably not make an ideal conductor. If, on the other hand, these problems seem vital and challenging in their possible application to a rehearsal situation, it may be assumed that he possesses at least one of the qualities essential to success. One who is not interested in numerical combinations could hardly be expected to be successful in mathematics or the physical sciences. By the same reasoning, one who lacks enthusiasm for melodic, harmonic, and rhythmic combinations could hardly be expected to succeed in a musical field in which these elements are basic.

Interesting musical combinations are found in the works of all composers; but few single works contain more, and more varied examples than may be found in the Goldmark overture *In Springtime*. Especially noteworthy is the passage which contains elements of the "confused rhythm" referred to earlier, together with the added complication of overlapping entrances, a difficulty which will be

considered in detail in succeeding paragraphs. Here may be found
the same slurred triplets against staccato duplets with overlapping
in these parts, and in addition, a solid rhythm in the bassoon and
harp parts. The skeleton score shows these patterns:

OVERTURE "IN SPRINGTIME" – GOLDMARK (Band)

(These parts are supported by other woodwind, and horn parts in the same rhythms.)
"In Springtime" used by permission of the publishers,
C.L.Barnhouse Co., Oskaloosa, Iowa

Independence, tempered with an appreciation of what other
players are doing, is the solution for this particular type of difficulty.
A helpful practice technique is to combine the flute, oboe, and bassoon, then the clarinets and bassoon, and finally all parts together.

The bassoon and harp parts might be played together merely for the purpose of illustrating the delightful simplicity and the beautiful coloring which these instruments contribute to the ensemble.

Goldmark makes use of the most intricate and interesting rhythmic devices to inject movement and excitement into his climactic passages, and the temptation to cite still another example from his overture *In Springtime* cannot be resisted. The following example will illustrate the technique:

OVERTURE "IN SPRINGTIME" – GOLDMARK (Band)

(The same rhythmic patterns are found in other voices.)
"In Springtime" used by permission of the publishers,
C. L. Barnhouse Co., Oskaloosa, Iowa

This excerpt embodies one fairly consistent basic rhythm in the horn parts, one rhythm which is based upon a triple accentuation in a two-beat measure (first cornet), the same rhythm and the same melody starting on the second beat of the measure instead of the first beat (baritone), and a fourth rhythm which does not fit exactly into either a duple or a triple pattern. The complexities of this passage can best be appreciated by playing each line alternately, bearing in mind that the tempo is vivace non troppo. In teaching the passage the only recourse is the tried and true method of very slow practice with exaggerated accents, one instrument at a time at first, then in various combinations. In such a difficult situation it is sometimes helpful to have a snare drummer beat six even beats to each measure as an accompaniment during the working-out process. This may impress some as a painfully slow method of mastering the rhythmic and technical difficulties of a composition, but this kind of practice pays big dividends in the end. It must not be forgotten that this sort of activity is all a part of the process of music education and that if the students were capable of playing the standard literature without this kind of drill, there would be no point in having school orchestras and bands, or even conductors and teachers.

Thus far in this investigation of ensemble technical problems the emphasis has been upon problems of rhythm, and there are several very good reasons why this should be the case. Rhythm is an indispensable part of music, and an analysis of the rhythmic elements in any given passage will usually furnish the key to an understanding of the passage in all of its essential aspects. A very wise teacher often tells his younger pupils that if they place the normal accents upon the right notes, the time will be correct. This is one of the most inflexible truths about music, and its general application should help students in their mastery of one of the more difficult phases of the art. To increase the student's sensitivity to all manner of rhythmic problems should be one of the first aims of the music teacher, and one means of achieving this desirable goal is to require a marked exaggeration of all accentuation where the rhythm or the counting constitutes a vital problem. "Understand the rhythm, and you will understand the tune" is one teacher's way of stressing the importance of this element, but no statement on the subject can equal in the force of its application the observation which has been attributed to

Robert Schumann, "The fingers cannot execute that which the brain does not thoroughly comprehend." Although rhythm is supposed to be closely allied to the emotions, it must also involve something of an intellectual process. If technic begins in the brain, so also does rhythm, at least where the practical instrumental performer is concerned. Hence it seems reasonable to expect that a most detailed study of all rhythmic problems involved in any difficult passage should be made before too much time is wasted in attempting to solve the technical problems by other and less effective means.

In band and orchestra literature one often finds passages which are difficult simply and solely because of the rapidity of sequence or the manner in which given passages must be fingered, bowed, or tongued. Such complexities may respond to individual practice and they may not. A number of successful conductors of school instrumental organizations have expressed the opinion, and have even proved the point in their own work, that almost no passage in the literature is too difficult for reasonably well-trained amateur players provided sufficient time is available for analysis, study, and practice. This means, of course, that the string parts must be properly marked with the correct bowings and fingerings, and that necessary alternate fingerings be indicated in the wind parts. With regard to certain passages, especially in the wind parts, which call for a range beyond the ordinary limits of the amateur, some rewriting of the score might be required to make good the claims of these ambitious conductors.

If it becomes a question of omitting an otherwise playable composition from the repertory because of an extremely difficult passage for a certain section, every usable device should be employed in order to raise the one section up to the level of the organization. Wagner's trick of writing a short, but difficult passage for the violins creates a problem for any conductor who might wish to play the *Meistersinger* Overture, for example. Similar passages occur in the *Flying Dutchman* and other of his works. Following is the passage from the *Die Meistersinger* Overture to which reference has been made:

OVERTURE "DIE MEISTERSINGER" -WAGNER (Orchestra)

This is strictly a technical difficulty, and there is no device which will insure its mastery without careful and conscientious practice by every member of the violin sections. There are, however, one or two suggestions which may help, chiefly as a means of keeping the students' interest in the passage alive until they have mastered its technical difficulties. First, the fingerings should be indicated. Those shown in the excerpt do not represent the only choice, but they keep the passage on the E string where it will be most brilliant. The next step is to "fill in" the quarter and eighth notes and rests with sixteenth notes in order to convert the passage into an exercise devoid of special bowing or rhythmic problems. The students should then be asked to play the passage with long, slow bows, forte. At about this point the difficulty of the skips will begin to appear, and this may be solved by playing such sequences as the following:

The same general idea may be applied to the mastery of the next shift (to the seventh position); and in order to firmly establish the entire sequence in the minds, ears, and fingers of the players it should be played in all of the ordinary rhythmic patterns, even including triplets and dotted rhythms, with and without special bowing forms. The passage might even be played *backwards*. Finally, the correct bowings should be used and every effort should be made to secure a full tone with a forceful, staccato bow stroke. This amount of detail is given only for the purpose of showing that practically nothing is impossible provided the inventive genius and the patience of the teacher are equal to the task.

Many seemingly difficult passages can be made intelligible, and hence playable, by a quite elementary analysis of the material in terms of the scale forms involved. This example, also from the *Meistersinger* Overture, will illustrate:

At first glance these runs appear difficult, but when they are found to be but parts of the E minor scale some of the mystery and confusion is dispelled. After some intensive work on the E minor scale itself, the problem will be largely solved. Incidentally, the first run may be worked out still more easily if the measure is completed as indicated and the subdivisions of the measure played in groups of one, two, and three notes as suggested by the short slur lines.

Earlier in this chapter the technique of coordination was discussed as a strictly mechanical problem — the problem of securing uniformity in the performance of two similar parts or two parts of the same melody played by different sections (see page 132). Accuracy in counting and adequacy in playing skill were stressed as the probable solutions of most difficulties of this type; but there is a slightly different phase of this question which is not easy to define and for which there does not appear to be any simple corrective device or procedure. The best examples of the problem are to be found in the more mature works of Wagner in which he assigns extremely flexible melodic material to various sections of the orchestra. These thematic bits are passed about in such manner that it is difficult for the players to coordinate them with other material and with the same material as stated by other sections, without losing some of their true significance. If these important themes are played in a strictly mechanical manner — with metronomic rigidity — they become musically meaningless, although to play them in this manner is infinitely easier. The chief problem, then, is: how to retain the desired flexibility and still remain within the framework of the conductor's beat. This involves the application of the principle of rubato, which is a problem both of expression and of mechanics. It is considered here as a phase of the general problem of coordination. The most obvious solution appears to be careful listening to the whole complex structure in order to correlate all melodic material and to emphasize that which is most significant. An exhaustive study of Wagner scores and recordings with this special problem in mind will reveal many interesting examples of coordinated playing under the most difficult of performing conditions. Material of this kind is, of course, far beyond the ability of most school organizations, but the problems which it presents will be found in modified form in the less difficult music which school groups are capable of playing.

The conductor will recognize that a very large part of the technical growth of his organization rests upon the solution of individual problems. The difficulties with which the player is confronted merge imperceptibly into the larger problems of the group, and it is sometimes impossible to distinguish between the two. In any case, such distinctions are of little importance since whatever means is used to remedy a situation operates for the benefit of all. Any attention given an individual in the rehearsal will, if the group is alert, react to the advantage of the entire group. Likewise, a drill procedure which may be applied to an entire section will benefit each member of that section and indirectly the orchestra or band as a whole. This is one of the great virtues of ensemble training.

In this chapter attention has been devoted chiefly to problems of group technique, and consequently no mention has been made of technical details which are of primary concern to the individual player. Some of these special technical considerations have been treated briefly in preceding chapters, but a practical knowledge of many of them can be acquired only in the private studio. For the conductor there is no distinction and no choice between group and individual problems. He must treat both equally within the limitations imposed upon him by the rehearsal situation.

A few of the technical problems which are individual in their application but which affect directly the work of the entire ensemble are: 1. the use of optional, or alternate, fingerings for the woodwind and valve instruments and the use of alternate positions on the trombone; 2. flexibility of the embouchure of brass players to permit the playing of the larger intervals with facility; 3. a knowledge of position work on the part of string players in order that all unnecessary difficulties may be avoided; 4. ability on the part of the tympani player to tune his instruments quickly and accurately; 5. facile tonguing on the part of all wind instrument players to insure a bright, lively playing style where this is required; 6. the ability on the part of all wind players to produce a fine, clean attack. These and many other purely technical elements enter into the group performance to such an extent that, if they have not been mastered previously, they must be regarded as legitimate material for group study and drill. Technical adequacy is essential to any worth-while performance, and if this can be developed only in the general rehearsal, the conductor must budget his time to include some group instruction and drill on the fundamental techniques.

The conductor may be able to save much valuable rehearsal time and add materially to the technical accomplishments of his players if he can succeed in teaching his players how to practice. No artist, however great his native talent, could have reached the heights of technical proficiency without first having learned this lesson. Methods of analysis and drill have been the basis of the success of such great master-teachers as Leopold Auer, and their pupils — the Elmans and Heifetzes, who have been compelled from the very earliest age to follow a strictly prescribed practice régime. These artists have achieved their goals not only by the *amount* of practice they have done, but also by their *methods* of practicing.

One of our leading band conductors states the problem well when he admonishes his students to "practice for results, not hours." To be of any value, the practice must be done on problems, not pieces. It should be the conductor's task to explain this method of practice and to point out in the rehearsal the particular passages which should be analyzed and mastered. One teacher follows the plan of having his students prepare ten single measures each day. They are expected to select these measures in the order of their difficulty and number them. The system has definite merit, for it develops in the student the habit of attacking the most difficult problem first. It leads to a mastery which can never be acquired by the system of practice usually employed, namely, "playing through" the lesson with all errors in counting, intonation, and technique repeated as many times as there are repetitions of the assigned material.

The conductor is charged with the responsibility of developing a well-rounded organization, and to accomplish this he must give due emphasis to technical growth along with other considerations. Any method which will prove effective in building better habits of accuracy in execution should be employed.

CHAPTER XIII

Tone Quality and Intonation

The artisan in any field should possess a thorough knowledge of the nature and structure of the materials with which he works. The carpenter should know his woods, the mason his stones and mortar, the tailor his fabrics, and the artist his pigments. It is no less important that the musician understand the fundamental character of the material with which he works. This material is *tone*, and it is a substance which can be created and controlled by the intelligent application of the laws of physics. The chief difficulty has always been, however, that the performing artist and the laboratory physicist have not been able to undersand one another or to agree either upon the basic laws or upon their application to the field of music.

The physicist has contributed learned and complex formulas for tone analysis and production, but he has failed to correlate this body of information with the requirements of the performer. The musician, on the other hand, leans toward the occult. Not knowing or caring much about the physical laws involved, he attributes tonal results to the traditional proportions and measurements of instruments which were evolved originally by artistic, utilitarian, and trial-and-error methods. Secret and mysterious varnishes and wood textures used in the making of string instruments are accepted as controlling factors without complete knowledge of their functions or proof of their actual effect. In the field of the wind instruments the texture and hardness of the metal, the diameter and shape of the bore, the depth and contour of the mouthpiece, and innumerable like considerations are accepted as guides in construction with very little truly scientific foundation.

On the technical side there is a similar lack of guidance based upon positive knowledge of physical laws. Tradition has played an important part both in the construction of instruments and in the manner of playing them, and in actual practice the musician depends upon what he hears and what he feels instead of upon what he knows about the instrument which he plays. This is not to suggest that the results of this approach have not been satisfactory from a musical standpoint; but the limited investigations which certain physicists and acousticians have undertaken suggest the possibility that a great many of the weaknesses which are apparent in tone production, tone control, and intonation may eventually find their solution through a more complete understanding of the science of sound.

The production of tone is basically an individual problem, depending upon the instrument itself and the manner in which it is played. The tone of an instrumental ensemble is built upon the tone of many individual players. If the tone produced by each of these individuals is of good quality and if each of the instruments is well in tune throughout its own range, the chances are that the ensemble tone will also be satisfactory. But in the ensemble a new set of problems arises — problems created by the combination of various types of instruments and instruments of the same kind having different basic tone qualities and peculiarities of pitch, tone production, and technique. The task is not wholly one of developing uniformity in these basic qualities, but of securing uniformity where this is desirable and contrast where a difference of dynamics, tone coloring, or style will serve a useful purpose in the interpretation of a given work.

The question of tone quality in the ensemble is frequently ignored in favor of the more obvious considerations of reading, interpretation, and technique; but good tone quality is probably as important to the ensemble as any of these other elements. It is more difficult to achieve, largely because the means of achieving it are not generally understood. Fundamentally, the production of a good ensemble tone depends upon three factors: correct intonation, proper dynamic balance, and uniformity of tone quality. Each of these three factors is important in some other way, but together they constitute the basis of good ensemble tone quality. Their other separate functions will be discussed in greater detail in later chapters.

The avoidance of faulty intonation is desirable primarily on the grounds that conflicting pitches are displeasing to the ear. There are correct discords, and these we accept; but a discord which is supposed to be a concord we cannot accept. This is the premise upon which most pleas for better intonation are based; but there is another which is of infinitely greater importance. This secondary consideration, which should be rightfully designated as the primary consideration, is based upon the theory of the reenforcement of overtones.

To comprehend the actual operation of the phenomenon one should have some slight knowledge of what is known as the "harmonic series of overtones." Like many things in music this is not as difficult as it sounds. The overtone series is simply that sequence of tones which may be produced by playing harmonics upon a stringed instrument, or the open tones upon a brass instrument. Following is a portion of the series which is playable upon the open C string of the cello:

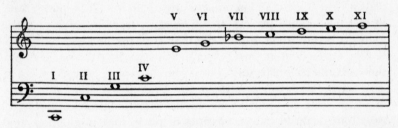

The open string C is, in this case, the fundamental. The second partial, or overtone, may be produced by touching the string lightly in its exact center between the head-nut and the bridge. The third partial responds when the string is touched one-third of the distance from either end, the fourth partial is heard when the segment is one-fourth of the string, and so on. The smaller the fractional part of the string, the higher is the partial tone which results. The interesting fact is that some or all of these partial tones are vibrating simultaneously with the fundamental tone whenever it is sounded; and the character of the composite tone which the listener hears is determined by the number, distribution, and relative strength of the partials present in the tone. These are facts which practically every instrumental conductor knows because all instruments utilize the harmonic series principle in their construction and technique. A great many conductors do not, however, appreciate the extent to which the principle of the harmonic series affects the tone of any ensemble.

The principle is based upon the fact that the natural overtones produced by one instrument serve to reenforce, or strengthen, either the fundamental tones or the overtones of every other instrument in the ensemble provided the instruments are in tune with one another. It must be borne in mind that there will be no reenforcement of tone unless the tuning is scientifically accurate. Approximate agreement in pitch will produce no sympathetic vibration whatever, nor will any amount of extra force bring about a response in another instrument. In fact, this approximation of the pitch produces just the opposite effect. One has only to listen to the resultant beats when two piano strings, one slightly higher than the other, are struck simultaneously to appreciate the full extent of the pitch disaster which results when six basses are tuned to six different pitches. The listener hears, not one set of dissonant beats, but several. The overtone series of each of these fundamental tones are vibrating in conflicting cycles throughout the audible pitch range, and the result is a wave of sound which is not recognizable as musical tone.

The application of the principle of sympathetic overtone vibration will be seen in the following illustration:

The open G string of the string bass, producing overtones of the actual pitches indicated above, contains three tones within the lower and middle portions of the harmonic series which are in agreement with tones in the partial series of the cello C string. These tones are enclosed in parentheses in both of the above overtone series. Still others, in the higher reaches of the series, might be faintly discernable under certain conditions. It will be observed that, of the common tones, the G appears twice in different octaves, and that the third common tone is a D.* This provides reenforcement for the fundamental tone of the bass (G) and the fifth of this fundamental (D), thereby strengthening the harmonic structure and providing as much extra force as might perhaps be supplied by an additional instrument. This reenforcement would actually occur whenever the open C string of the cello were sounded against the open G string of the bass, and a similar, but not identical, reenforcement would be present in every combination of tones by all of the various instru-

---

* See John Redfield's *Music: A Science and an Art* pages 45 to 50 on exclusion of certain partials.

ments. The only condition demanded is that the instruments be in tune with one another and that they be played in tune.

Actually, it is not possible to tune any organization with sufficient accuracy to insure complete sympathy and perfect resonance; but this is the ideal toward which every organization should strive. It is not likely that even professionals will always play with sufficient agreement in pitch to induce the theoretical maximum of resonance. Intonation is relative, ranging from that which is so poor that the actual pitch discrepancies can be easily recognized by the non-musician to that in which the only trace of false pitch is an occasional flurry of beats between the wind instruments or the "squeal" of violins in the higher register. The intonation of a very large group of amateur players may be measured not so much by actual audible dissonance as by a mass of indistinguishable sound — a sort of rumbling undertone of noise — which represents a composite of dissonance. The well-tuned professional group, on the other hand, may be distinguished by the clarity of its melodic and harmonic outline. This device of measuring, or rather estimating, the intonational status of an organization by the degree of tonal clarity is fairly reliable. One conductor has described the characteristic undercurrent of noise which is heard when a group is badly out of tune as "musical mud." This is an apt term. One might wonder why it is that amateur organizations sound as well as they sometimes do in view of the poor intonation which is known to exist. This may be explained by the fact that all of the instruments which are in agreement in the matter of pitch reenforce one another and thus fuse into a mass tone which is much stronger than the single instruments that vary from this dominant pitch standard. There is much more to be said on this subject of intonation, but for the present the second of the elements which contribute to a satisfactory ensemble tone quality must be considered. This is the element of dynamic balance. The question of dynamic treatment for expressive and other specific purposes will be considered elswhere in greater detail, but its importance as a factor in the building of ensemble tone merits more than passing mention.

Unless a particular instrument is treated as a solo instrument, or unless the character of the harmony is such that one tone should predominate over all others, a correct balance of tonal force is indicated. Cornet tone accompanied by other brass instruments is one thing, but equal brass parts sounding together is something entirely different. The two should not be confused by carelessness in the treatment of individual voices. The problem being considered is that of securing ensemble tone, and it must be perfectly obvious that without ceaseless attention to the matter of dynamic balance, the playing of the band would be characterized by a series of chords in which first one instrument and then another would stand out as solo voices. This practice would never result in the production of chords which possessed the distinctive ensemble coloring and quality. A dynamic overbalance in favor of one instrument not only gives the chord the character of that particular instrument, but it also disturbs the blend of the chord by overemphasizing certain of the overtones at the expense of the others. Another and equally important reason for maintaining a correct dynamic balance is that this permits all of the players to hear the composition of the chord more easily; and this, in turn, should lead to more careful tuning and more concentration upon the analysis of tone quality.

It is in this matter of tone quality that many amateur organizations fall below an acceptable standard, and again the cause is largely the neglect of detail. Ensemble tone is a mixture of a large number of ingredients. If these are of good quality, and the correct ingredients, the resultant concoction will be palatable; but if one of a foreign character finds its way into the mixture, the flavor will suffer. This simile does not represent an exaggeration of the facts. To put salt into the pudding instead of sugar is no worse in the final reckoning than to include two or three clarinet players whose tone is coarse and raucous in a section in which all other players produce a beautiful tone. Strangely enough, the tone of the two or three will predominate *because it is different,* and the tonal level of the entire section will drop accordingly. The principle of fused tone does not apply in the matter of quality. Most conductors are in the habit of stressing tone quality in the smaller sections where the tone can be heard more distinctly for what it is or what it is not; but very often these same conductors fail to search out the perpetrators of tonal misdeeds in the larger sections. This matter of blend or balance in tone quality may refer back to what has been said earlier concerning the mechanical condition of the instruments, but it also has an important relationship to the manner in which the instruments are played. For example, it has been shown that both velvet and sandpaper are present within the quality range of most instruments, and there are legitimate places for both within the expressional limits of instrumental music. The important matter for the conductor to watch is that particular students do not get their interpretative signals confused and supply a sandpaper tone against a velvet background. There are even a few occasions on which the player of an individual instrument will be called upon to produce a tone the quality of which approximates that of another instrument. A rare example of this may be found in the Hindemith *Quintet* (Op. 24, No. 2) for woodwind instruments, in which a descending flute figure is taken up by the bassoon in its upper register. In the hands of skilled players this bridge of tone between two normally dissimilar instruments can be executed with an almost perfect matching of tone quality.

There are many items of interest in connection with this question of blended quality, or contrasted quality, but none is of greater importance than that of so-called "solo" quality as opposed to "accompanying" quality. In the absence of any scientific data on the subject it must be assumed that there are two principal elements of contrast which account for the fact that the professional instrumentalist is able to project his solo passages with apparent ease, even though the accompanying background is fairly involved. One factor is undoubtedly that of dynamics. The soloist plays somewhat louder than do those on the accompanying parts, but one always has the feeling that loudness is not his principal resource. The unskilled player is likely to rely upon dynamic force as the chief means of projecting his tone, whereas the experienced professional musician accomplishes the same purpose by producing a distinctive quality, or character, of tone. This solo tone, which may be described as having a more compact resonance and an added richness and vitality, is easily heard against a tonal background which lacks these characteristics. Incidentally, it is important that players assigned to accompanying parts avoid, in large measure, the use of the "solo type" tone. An apt parallel may be drawn here between ensemble music and the graphic arts, in both of which care must be exerted not to obscure the principal features by over-emphasis on background material. This principal of contrast in tone color, which serves so useful a purpose in ensemble music, has its roots in a complete understanding on the part of the player, of the technical and musical possibilities of his instrument. In the string section both contrast and uniformity may be obtained through the regulation of the vibrato, but until the technical background of the vibrato becomes somewhat more uniform for the wind instruments, this control factor must be utilized with extreme caution by the players in the wind group. It must be recognized that the peculiarly "alive" tone which wind players use in the playing of solo passages may, and usually does, involve an application of the vibrato principle. The contrast between a vital tone and a "dead" tone is best illustrated on the stringed instruments; the fingered tone, either with or without the vibrato, representing the former and the open string tone, the latter.

Before undertaking a further analysis of the difficulties involved in securing satisfactory ensemble intonation, mention should be made of one peculiar characteristic of the wind instruments which has a direct bearing upon the related problems of tone quality and intonation.

Earlier it was stated that a certain amount of variation in the pitch of any given note is possible on all of the wind instruments. This pitch variation is controlled by the embouchure of the player, and almost all professional instrumentalists accept this principle as a basic condition of playing with others, recognizing it as the only means of controlling intonation. A few sombre souls still believe that they can get the pitch from a tuning bar and hold it through thick and thin. The interesting fact about the variable pitch phenomenon is that the quality of the tone varies as much as does the pitch. The lower pitch is produced with an extremely loose embouchure and the same adjective describes the resultant tone. It lacks quality, it includes much more of the breath sound, and it does not carry well. At the other pitch extreme the exact opposite occurs. The tightening of the embouchure permits the passage of less air, and the tone has a pinched, muted quality. This contrast can probably be explained entirely upon the basis of the release or restriction of overtone vibrations resulting from an improper balance between breath supply and lip vibration with reference to a fixed length of tubing. Somewhere about midway between these extremes in pitch and quality range may be found the ideal tone quality, and since any downward or upward deviation from this mean is sure to involve a sacrifice both in quality and in flexibility, the wind instruments should be so tuned that the players will be required to make only minor pitch adjustments.

As was suggested in connection with the discussion of group intonation earlier in this chapter, a certain amount of "spread" in the pitch of any ensemble must be expected. The problem is to hold this spread down to a minimum and to guard against any tendency to exaggerate the discrepancies in intonation. Having touched briefly upon the subject of the vibrato, it might be well to consider its effect upon the intonation of the group.

There are two principal types of vibrato: the *pitch* vibrato and the *intensity* vibrato. Since the latter has no direct effect upon intonation it may be disregarded for the purpose of this discussion. Following are four representations of ensemble tone which may serve to illustrate the practical problems involved in securing perfect pitch:

A

(A) represents a purely hypothetical case—an orchestra or a band which is perfectly in tune. Every instrument follows the pitch line exactly; there is no deviation and no vibrato.

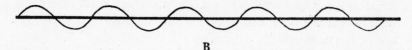

B

(B) shows this perfect pitch being disturbed by the use of vibrato. The vibrato is, essentially, playing out of tune—alternating above and below the line of fixed pitch. The ear tends to accept the mean pitch (represented by the straight line) and to disregard the variations from this pitch, unless the variations become too extensive or too slow.

C

(C) suggests another hypothetical situation—an organization in which most of the players are in agreement or near-agreement, but in which several have wandered above or below the fixed standard. Viewed at close range the discrepancies in these pitch lines can be easily seen, but from a greater distance those which are near together in the center fuse into a single solid line. The same illusion is registered upon the ear when a large number of instruments produce an *approximate* unison. In this illustration the group uses no vibrato, but the effect will be fairly satisfactory because of the predominant weight of tone on the mean pitch.

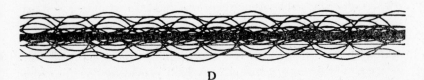

D

(D) represents the same group of players using the out-of-tune vibrato. On the principle that the ear does not discern with any great fidelity the variations from the mean pitch, the playing of this group would be fairly acceptable to the listener, although lacking the clarity represented by illustrations A, B, and C, even though some players are out of tune and all are utilizing the out-of-tune vibrato technique.

The spreading, overlapping, and wholly irregular effect shown in the last illustration will be heard by the discerning listener as the "musical mud" referred to above (page 154), but in spite of the basic pitch discrepancies and the general flux in the ensemble tone resulting from the use of vibrato, the mean pitch is still the predominant one and will usually assert itself over the foggy background of dissonance. It is upon the basis of this type of analysis that we find the explanation of the difference between tonal clarity and tonal obscurity in ensemble performance. With some concentration and practice in analysis, the auditor can evaluate these elements, and can form a rough estimate of the degree to which good intonation has been achieved, by weighing these conflicting elements of tonal clarity and tonal obscurity. The dissonant elements — poor tuning of instruments, playing off pitch, using excessive vibrato — might be represented, as in the following illustration, by the clouded area above and below the solid line. The thickness and clarity of this line representing the dominant pitch will vary according to the *proportion* of instruments playing in absolute, or approximate unison.

While these illustrations are entirely unscientific, they do illustrate graphically some rather interesting facts concerning group performance. If all of the faulty intonation present in the playing of instrumental ensembles, both amateur and professional, were transmitted to the listener with full impact, public interest in this form of art would terminate abruptly. A kind providence has protected the auditor from the ill effects of all but the most obvious pitch discrepancies, and unless one is trained to listen for the more subtle evidences of a basically faulty intonation, he can accept the average performance with fortitude, if not with enthusiasm. Certain of our acoustical scientists* have isolated this phenomenon and have explained a few of the reasons for our insensibility to pitch discrepancies. The recognition of these facts should encourage those who deal with amateurs, but it should not condone poor workmanship or laxity in the conductor's struggle against the ogre of false pitch.

The vibrato has long been a favored device for obscuring faulty intonation. Soloists in all fields have used it most effectively, as have string quartets and the larger ensembles. This is not, however, the sole function of the vibrato. It serves a useful purpose in giving vitality to the ensemble tone and in adding a touch of smoothness to a melodic line or a harmony which would otherwise stand out in too sharp relief. To use the vibrato most effectively in all fields — expression, tone quality, intonation — would seem to be a perfectly legitimate practice; and if science has shown the conductor an acceptable use of the vibrato as a palliative for the distress of false pitch, why not make intelligent use of this device? The vibrato should, however, be employed in conjunction with the most exacting instruction and drill in interval and chord relationships, and it

* Dean Carl E. Seashore, and associates, of the State University of Iowa.

should not be used as a substitute for this type of careful and constructive work.

To illustrate in still another way the effect of faulty intonation,
poor balance, and the absence of that quality which has been referred to as "blend," another form of graphic representation has been
invented. This is designed to illustrate visually as nearly as possible
the aural effect of various types of performance upon one who not
only hears an instrumental performance with a sensitive and critical
ear but who also understands the technical and mechanical forces
which operate to produce the different tonal effects.

In the following graphs the parallel horizontal lines represent the
basic harmonic structure of the ensemble or, in this case, the accompaniment. Superimposed upon these lines is a single variable line
which indicates the solo voice, or the principal theme, whether
played by one instrument or several. Dynamic values are indicated
by the thickness or weight of the lines. Breath pauses and like interruptions in the flow of tone are shown by breaks in the lines.

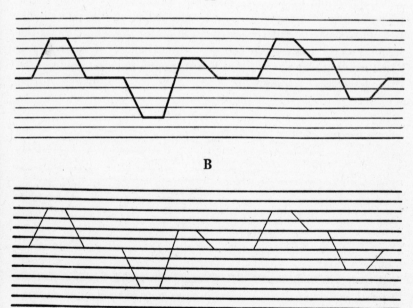

A

B

This illustrative device is employed to show three different types of ensemble performance, the merits or demerits of which may be easily identified.

(A) represents a performance which is highly accurate in all respects—good intonation, satisfactory balance between parts in the accompaniment, and most important, a melodic line which stands out clearly above the accompanying voices.

(B) illustrates a somewhat less satisfactory performance resulting from lack of attention to the problem of balance. Here the solo voice becomes lost in the too ponderous accompaniment. While the general outline of the melody can be traced, it does not stand out with sufficient clarity to be easily identified. The most successful performance will be that in which the various elements are easily distinguished by the listener. The principal melody should stand out sharply from the accompaniment, counter-melodies should also be near the threshold of attention, and there should be no uncertainty as to the nature of the harmonic structure. The moment the listener is forced to concentrate intensively upon the music in order to grasp all of its essential elements he begins to lose his enjoyment of the performance. Listening should be easy. Unless both melody and harmony elicit an instantaneous recognition and identification, the listener, in his attempt to deliberate or reconstruct a doubtful passage, will lose the significance of that which follows. Music moves—it is not static like a painting or a statue—and hence, its full import must register at the moment of passing.

C

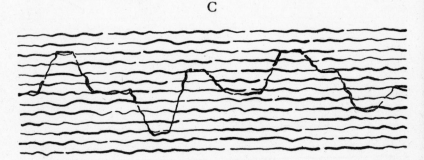

Example (C) illustrates a performance in which faults in matters of pitch, dynamics, and sostenuto predominate to such an extent that all clarity and form are destroyed.

Many amateur performances actually do give about the same confused impression to the ear that this formless pattern conveys to the eye. The remedy, however, is not hard to find. It is largely a matter of reorganizing the materials already at hand and bringing order out of seeming chaos. A little careful analysis, some drill on fundamentals of tone production and control, greater emphasis upon listening and cross-checking of results, perhaps a few minor repairs or adjustments of the instruments, and the clear light of form, proportion, and beauty will begin to penetrate the murky haze of dissonance and distortion. As the corrective process advances, however, it will be discovered that intonation looms as perhaps the greatest single obstacle to the attainment of the desired objective.

To alter a quotation which has enjoyed wide circulation in recent years: Eternal vigilance is the price of good intonation. This vigilance cannot be effective unless the conductor knows where to look for difficulties and how to correct them after they have been discovered. He must be a relentless foe of false intonation, a stern judge of standards, but a patient and painstaking counselor.

There are four main categories to which almost all faults in intonation may be assigned. These are as follows:

1. Pitch discrepancies between individuals within the larger sections, such as the violin section in the orchestra and the clarinet section in the band. This type of intonation difficulty is distinguished by a generally noisy tone and lack of clarity.

2. Pitch discrepancies between individual players in the smaller sections or between individuals in several of the smaller sections. This pitch "spread" is heard for what it is—a direct conflict in tonality.

3. Pitch discrepancies between the principal sections, the instruments within each section being fairly well in tune with one another. This is a common fault and one which is most disconcerting to the listener. In tutti passages the melody, harmony, and even the rhythm are effectively obliterated, and in passages featuring the separate sections the constantly shifting pitch destroys the effectiveness of the entire performance.

4. Pitch discrepancies within the range of single instruments. This type of false pitch is most noticeable in solo passages, but if prevalent throughout an organization, it can be the means of keep-

ing the entire group in a condition of uncertainty and indecision in the matter of tonality.

From what has been stated earlier concerning the technical problems of the various instruments and the effect of mechanical considerations upon intonation, it should be obvious that the correction of the type of pitch discrepancy mentioned last must rest upon more careful individual work. The conductor must contribute his oversight and his guidance, but the inability to play scales and intervals in tune is essentially an individual problem and must always remain such.

All of the other types of pitch trouble depend for their correction upon the discovery or utilization of some method of general tuning which will insure reasonably satisfactory results in bringing all sections and all individuals into common agreement. This system must be positive in its results, it must operate without too much loss of rehearsal time, and it must function with equal effectiveness outside the regular rehearsal hall or wherever the organization may be required to play.

The prevailing standard pitch is 440 vibrations per second for the A above middle C, and in theory this should settle all questions about the basic pitch of orchestras and bands. In practice, however, the A-440 is more likely to be a point of departure. Temperature and humidity affect the pitch of the instruments in varying degrees. Some instruments are being constructed on a pitch standard above the A-440 to meet the requirements of radio and professional groups, other instruments used in school organizations are below the A-440 level, and still others range from A-430 to A-450, depending upon which tones in the range of the particular instrument are sounded.

Perhaps the best first step in establishing a fixed pitch for an organization is to provide a standard tuning bar (A for orchestra and B-flat for the band) and to suspend this where it can be used conveniently by all of the players. If possible, this should be regarded as the basic pitch and any instruments which are below this pitch should be either repaired in such manner as to remedy the defect or replaced by standard instruments. Any instruments that are above the fixed pitch should be adjusted to bring them down to the level of the group. The real difficulty arises when it is discovered that there are several important instruments which are below the fixed pitch, with no possibility of replacing or repairing these instruments. It is at this point that the tuning bar becomes practically useless, and it may as well be discarded except as a device for keeping the instruments at least in approximate agreement. Under these conditions, the conductor must determine which of the instruments is the "problem child" and this one will determine the pitch level of the entire group. The conductor must bear in mind, however, that such a radical step should be taken only after every resource for bringing the particular instrument up to pitch has been exhausted.

Another condition which will probably nullify the effect of the tuning bar is that of extremely warm weather or abnormally high temperature in the rehearsal or concert hall. Groups which rehearse during the summer months can seldom keep down to the pitch of the tuning bar without pulling all of the wind instruments and thus causing even greater pitch and intonation difficulties. Under such circumstances it seems better to permit the pitch of the entire group to rise than to attempt to adhere to an arbitrary standard. In fact, this theory of a fluctuating pitch has practical advantages which must be recognized. While a fine professional symphony orchestra, playing under controlled atmospheric conditions and equipped with the finest standard instruments, might be able to maintain a fixed pitch, this is usually not possible for the average amateur organization. The important consideration must always be that the group remain in tune with itself.

Assuming that a reasonable amount of unison tuning is necessary to establish a common pitch, a word of warning on the subject might be admissible. This process can easily become not only a waste of time but a very bad joke which the conductor and the students play upon one another. The player unconsciously acquires skill in "matching tones"; and with this method of tuning he merely matches the tuning bar or the tone played by another student, while his instrument remains essentially out of tune. Either this, or the tuning note might be out of tune with the remainder of his instrument. There also remains the difficulty of matching tuning notes in different octaves and with contrasting tone qualities.

In view of the doubtful results likely to be obtained from this method of tuning, it would seem best to rely almost exclusively upon some method of chord tuning in which the various instruments retain a proper relationship in matters of range and distribution of harmony. One such method * employs unison tones for the rough preliminary tuning, then simple triads and seventh chords, the more common major and minor scales in unison, a harmonized diatonic and chromatic scale, and an easy chorale-type tune for the final check on the intonation of the ensemble. In these arrangements each section is treated as a unit and the testing of intonation may be done by sections alone or in any combination. One virtue of such a method is that the extreme limits of the tonal range of the instrument are treated in the chords and in the unison scales. Many organizations which can play well in tune in the middle registers fail completely when the range extremities are employed.

To correct a fault mentioned earlier in this chapter, i.e., the pitch spread between sections, the most practical device seems to be the creation of a pitch-conscious nucleus — an organization within an organization. Since most of the difficulties of this type concern the wind instruments, this special group might include the first chair players of the flute, oboe, bassoon, clarinet, French horn, cornet, and trombone sections of the orchestra, and in the band the same players plus the first alto saxophone and the first tuba. Within this group may be found various types of small wind ensembles, and if some careful ensemble playing is done by these players, many of the pitch problems of the band and the orchestra will be eliminated. Under the operation of this plan the first chair player must accept a two-way responsibility. He will be responsible for keeping in tune with the other first chair players and he will endeavor to keep his own section in tune with himself and with one another. In the same manner, the principal string players should be encouraged to do small ensemble work and to maintain a close pitch relationship at all times.

The battle against faulty intonation will be half won when the conductor succeeds in establishing a pitch-consciousness throughout his organization. This cannot be achieved merely by talking about pitch, or even by devoting rehearsal time to the ordinary tuning practices. The players must be led into a deeper appreciation of the value of fine intonation by having their attention called to any chord which is perfectly blended and tuned. Such a chord has a character which is entirely different from that of a chord which is not well in tune, in which individual voices stand out above the others, or in

---

* Righter-Dasch Tuning Method for Orchestra; Righter-Grabel Tuning Method for Band.

which the tone quality is not uniform. An ideal of fine intonation must be established before amateur players will even be moved to make the effort necessary to attain such an ideal.

There are a number of interesting devices which may prove helpful in establishing a listening attitude. These are, in a sense, pitch games. Most of them rely for their success upon the ability of the individual player to modify the pitch of his instrument upward or downward in order to bring a given tone into agreement with tones being sounded by other instruments. One of the more simple of these devices is to have two players of the same type instrument play a scale in thirds. One player starts on the tonic, the other on the third, and both play a full octave scale in whole notes. The player who starts on the third of the scale must be instructed to adjust the pitch of each tone he plays to that of the other player, and the intervals must be sustained until there is perfect pitch agreement. The result is obvious. At various points in the scale very marked adjustments are required, and for the first time the members of the group begin to understand what the conductor means by pitch modification.

A somewhat more spectacular device is one designed to prove that instruments which are out of tune with one another may be *played* in tune. The first step is to tune three cornets as carefully as possible, testing all of the tones of the scale and finally having the three players sound a single C–E–G triad. This triad should be built from the lowest note, and in this process there may be some slight pitch adjustment. This is merely incidental, however. The next step is to pull all of the valve slides and the tuning slides of the instruments which sounded the E and the G of the chord. The slides should not be pulled too much, but enough to make the horns definitely out of tune with themselves and with one another. The final step is to build the triad as before, except that this time each player will find it necessary to make a very marked adjustment of pitch. The triad can be made to sound perfectly in tune, however, and the students will have proved to themselves that the ear and the lip are the principal factors in securing correct intonation.

The vigilance of the conductor will take many forms. He will test odd combinations of instruments where he suspects some faulty intonation, he will call for a test of octaves upon single instruments, he will ask individual students to play scales in keys which will show the least satisfactory intonation, and he will single out odd chord structures for special testing. All conductors recognize, of course, that the string pitch is depressed as the room temperature rises and that the wind pitch rises with the thermometer. This suggests the advisability of having the strings tune slightly above the desired pitch at the start of the rehearsal. Special care should also be exercised in keeping the lower strings in tune. It is more often than not the D and the G strings of the violins which go out of tune unnoticed, and the same is true of the G and C strings of the viola and the cello. The string bass is difficult to tune throughout its range, and because of this fact many conductors have their string bass players tune in a separate room, away from the noise and confusion of the other instruments.

One of the peculiar problems of the clarinets is that, in the production of a crescendo, the pitch tends to go down. On the brass instruments the exact opposite occurs. Naturally, a rather serious pitch spread will result whenever these two types of instruments execute a crescendo, unless all of the players make a conscious effort to compensate for the normal pitch variation. This acoustical phenomenon can be demonstrated by having first one section and then the other play the crescendo on the same pitch. If the same tone is then played by the two sections simultaneously, the discrepancy in pitch will usually be quite obvious. The remedy rests in developing the habit of pitch compensation.

Another of the more common causes of faulty intonation is a variation of the temperature control problem mentioned in the preceding paragraph. If the temperature of the room in which the orchestra or band plays is lower than the normal playing temperature of the wind instruments, there is the tendency for the instruments to cool during any rest periods in the performance and consequently to become lower in pitch. After an extended rest period, the individual student starts to play with his instrument flat in pitch. As he continues, the instrument warms gradually, and during this warming-up process the tones produced by the warm end of the instrument are sharp while those produced by the cool end of the instrument are flat. This applies chiefly to the woodwind instruments. The answer, in this case, is for the player to blow warm air through his instrument throughout all extended rest periods, or at least at sufficiently frequent intervals to maintain a constant temperature at the playing level.

No major task in the field of instrumental group performance is ever quite completed. The architect or the builder may view his work in finished form, but this goal is never attained by the conductor of an amateur orchestra or band. Even though he may present a concert which has cost him and the members of his group weeks of painstaking work, this concert merely serves to emphasize the technical and musical shortcomings of individual players and to point the way to more study and more practice in preparation for future concerts. This is not a discouraging outlook. It is the condition under which the truly qualified teacher thrives best. It is a living, growing situation in which progress rather than fixed attainment provides the measurement of values. The factors in this situation are far too varied and variable to be classified, catalogued, and then controlled by some specific operation or device which is certain to produce the desired result. The instrumental rehearsal is not a factory with its production line so much as it is a laboratory in which endless experiments are undertaken, some of which turn out successfully and others of which fail completely. This uncertainty as to method and procedure applies, in a degree, to all phases of instrumental music training, but on the question of intonation each teacher or conductor must be a law unto himself. One can only suggest and advise — the final results will depend upon the discernment and the resourcefulness of the individual teacher.

CHAPTER XIV

Balance and Dynamic Contrast

Music is such a complex art that it is extremely difficult to separate its various elements even for convenience in studying them. One cannot discuss ensemble tone quality, for example, without considering the importance of dynamic balance. Problems of instrumental technique frequently find their solution in an exaggeration of accent, which is a form of dynamic treatment. Expression and interpretation depend very largely upon technique, tone color, and control of tonal intensity. These different elements interlock and overlap to such an extent that even the performer himself might be confused if he were asked to define in exact terms the actual process involved in producing a given musical effect. This may explain, in large measure, the subjective character of the art as practiced by many soloists and the failure of even some of the finest performers when they enter the field of teaching. Careful analysis must always precede an exposition on any subject as involved as that of cause and effect in musical performance, and even after the most detailed preliminary study one often finds that his deductions have been based upon false premises.

Of one fact concerning the subject of dynamic balance, however, we may be reasonably certain, and this fact is that *tonal intensity* is the one controllable element upon which all harmonic and melodic clarity must finally depend. The reasons for this should be apparent. First among the considerations which serve to emphasize the fundamental importance of tonal balance is the instrumentation of the orchestra and the band. By definition these groups may be said to be "balanced" groups of musical instruments. Why does the standard orchestra contain, for example, sixteen first violins, twelve violas, three flutes, three trombones, and a more or less fixed complement of the other instruments? The obvious reason is that this number and distribution of instrumental voicing have proved to be most satisfactory over a long period and that this tonal balance satisfies most of the ordinary requirements. Another factor which establishes the fundamental importance of dynamic balance is the use which is made of this instrumentation. Technical facility and beauty of expression mean nothing unless presented to the listener in audible and understandable form, and this depends entirely upon considerations of tonal balance. Music is fundamentally an art built upon contrast. A melody consists of high tones and low tones, long tones and short tones. The beauty and force of an instrumental ensemble rests upon contrast in the tone color of the various instruments. Musical forms present a contrast in meter and tempo. And finally, contrast in volume of sound, or tonal intensity, must be regarded as of basic importance. These are only the most obvious elements of contrast upon which the art of music is based, but of these, dynamic contrast is probably the one which enters most subtly into the fabric of the instrumental ensemble and gives true meaning to most of the other basic media of expression. If one may judge by the relatively large amount of rehearsal time which the conductor usually devotes to problems of tonal intensity, this would seem to be one of the most important elements in both the mechanical and the interpretative aspects of ensemble performance.

What are the most fundamental uses and functions of this technical and expressive agency which may be referred to variously as dynamic balance, dynamic contrast, total intensity, volume of sound, accent or pulsation?

In the preceding chapter the relationship between the intensity of tone of individual instruments and the larger element of ensemble tone quality was discussed in some detail. No mention was made, however, of one of the most significant uses of tonal force, that is, the determination of harmonic character through stress upon a particular note in the chordal structure. This function is recognized by the conductors of symphony orchestras, members of string quartets and among the better professional players in all fields. The method is quite simple, involving as it does only an added degree of dynamic force on the tone, or tones, which give a chord its special character. For example, in a major triad it is the major third which is the important tone, in a minor triad it is the minor third, and in a dominant seventh chord the tones to be stressed are the major third and the minor seventh. If the characteristic tones in a succession of chords are overbalanced by less important tones in these chords, the effect is still that of a series of different harmonies, but the relationship of these harmonies is entirely lost upon the listener, and the sequence lacks color, force, and interest. If, on the other hand, the principal tone is properly stressed, even a single sustained chord or a simple cadence will be musically satisfying. The stressed tone in one chord will normally progress to a stressed tone in the succeeding chord, and hence the entire harmonic sequence is enhanced and enriched.

The objection may be raised that the average student does not possess sufficient knowledge of harmony to provide a proper basis for this form of dynamic treatment, and this is probably true in most cases. It then becomes the task of the conductor to point out to the players the most essential tones to be stressed — not in every chord, but in those passages in which chordal coloring is most important — and to encourage the players to make their own choices. This problem emphasizes the desirability and utility of more careful listening and more active participation by the individual player in the business of making the music interesting. If the untrained members of a "barbershop" quartet can discover by trial-and-error methods the tones to be stressed in a harmonic progression, certainly the members of an orchestra or a band can do this, unless they have had their native musical instincts trained out of them through an inflexibly rigid program of note-reading. Any performance which is dull and stolid due to the neglect of this important matter of harmonic stress may be vastly improved by the rather simple device of urging the players to emphasize any tone in the chord which they themselves feel may add color and interest to the harmony. Their intelligence and musical feeling will provide a reasonably safe guide, and practice in listening will lead to a gradual improvement in this important phase of interpretation.

Balance and contrast between melody and accompaniment should not require special consideration, as it would seem to be one of the most obvious elements in musical performance, but in actual practice this vital problem is seldom solved to the entire satisfaction of the listener. The solution appears to be quite simple when stated as an academic problem in tonal balance. The melody must be played louder than the accompaniment. But the solution is not to be found so easily. Carrying power depends upon elements of contrast as much as upon relative volume of tone, and the nature or character of both melody and accompaniment is another important factor. No two problems are identical and no two solutions will apply with exactly the same degree of effectiveness. This general problem, more than almost any other which the conductor may be called upon to face, requires for its solution an extremely sensitive ear and practiced judgment as to the relative weight of any and all combinations of instruments in every conceivable style of instrumental writing. In most scores no attempt is made to differentiate between the volume of the various instruments, and even where some distinction is made these dynamic markings constitute only a rough guide. Actually, the players and the conductor must work this problem out in the rehearsal on the basis of tone quality, range, volume, harmonic density, complexity of inner voices, and the acoustical properties of the rehearsal hall.

One of the most practical rules to be followed in seeking a solution of the melody-accompaniment problem is that the melody should be played one dynamic degree *louder* than indicated in the part and that the accompaniment should be played one dynamic degree *softer* than indicated. (See graphs and explanatory matter on pages 161 to 163.) Assuming that both or all parts bear the marking mezzo forte, the melody should be played forte and the accompaniment piano. This might seem to provide too much contrast in volume, but actually it does not, probably because of the fact that there may be more instruments assigned to accompanying parts than to the melody. One of the chief virtues of this rule is that it suggests to the student that he himself is the one to decide which of the musical material is melody and which is accompaniment. It is of the utmost importance that the members of the group be trained to make decisions of this nature. The rehearsals are not long enough for the conductor to point out every dynamic indication, every key change, and every mark of expression or tempo. The advancement of the group is determined largely by the number and importance of the special items for which the players assume major responsibility. An organization in which the members themselves know when to subdue the accompaniment, bring out the melody, or stress particular tones in certain chords may be regarded as having approached professional excellence. This individual and group responsiveness to the details of technic and interpretation will always be reflected in the performance of the organization.

One of the minor complexities of dynamic treatment concerns the handling of melodic material in the inner or accompanying voices. A good example of this occurs in the following excerpt:

SYMPHONY No. V IN E MINOR – LARGO – DVORAK (Orchestra)

(Partial score only.)

By permission of Associated Music Publishers, Inc., New York.

Here the solo is taken by the English horn, but there are very short fragments of melody in the accompanying string parts, sometimes amounting to little more than a harmonic change in one voice or a group of passing tones. These may be regarded as secondary melodic material and they should be stressed sufficiently to be heard above the other string parts. Such passages will seldom intrude upon the principal solo because the attention of the listener is fixed on the solo, and because the accompanying voices present a less penetrating quality of tone. For these reasons there is little likelihood of such parts being over-stressed. Usually they will not be brought out with sufficient force.

In both orchestra and band the treatment of tutti passages which call for the fortissimo in all parts is frequently a travesty upon the musical art. As often as not, especially among younger groups, the entire character of the organization changes whenever one of these passages is encountered. An orchestra, for example, which is well-balanced in piano and mezzo forte passages, suddenly becomes a brass band! All thought of orchestral balance is forsaken and the brasses (and percussion) take over completely. The reason for this is obvious; the brasses command a much greater tonal power than the strings and the woodwinds combined. There are, nevertheless, remedies which the conductor should employ in maintaining at least a semblance of orchestral balance.

The brasses should be instructed to modify the dynamic force of the fortissimo in all such passages, and the other sections must be taught and trained to extend their power to the utmost limit. Most amateur string and woodwind players have neglected to develop a good fortissimo, and they instinctively withdraw from any attempt to match the brasses in this field. As a result they, as a group, fail to supply a quality of tone which must be an essential part of the orchestral fortissimo. It becomes the function of the strings and the woodwinds to "fill in" the lower and inner harmonies and to supply a rich body of overtones which have the effect of modifying the blare of the higher brasses. Especially is this phenomenon of tonal mixture important in the band. The "brassy" quality of the fortissimo climaxes can be obliterated entirely and replaced by a resonant mass of tone suggestive of the full organ if all of the woodwind players can be prevailed upon to contribute the maximum volume consistent with reasonable standards of quality and intonation. The conductor of the band may solve this problem by building the fortissimo in his woodwind section first, and then superimposing the brass sections upon this solid foundation of tone. These suggestions do not apply, of course, to such passages as are designed to feature the brass instruments above the remainder of the ensemble. Where the brasses are clearly intended to dominate the tonal picture, no attempt should be made to subdue their part or to match it in intensity with string or woodwind tone.

At the opposite dynamic pole, the conductor will occasionally experience some difficulty in obtaining an evenly distributed pianissimo. In fact, many conductors fail to educe from their organizations a pianissimo of any description. To play softly and still control the quality and the pitch and at the same time maintain an even intensity of tone requires an almost professional skill of the individual, and to secure this same response throughout an organization demands unusual patience on the part of the conductor. What few realize is the destructive effect which one or two instruments may have upon the ensemble pianissimo. Almost the entire clarinet section of the band, or string section of the orchestra, may be producing a superb pianissimo tone, but if there is one player in the group who is either unwilling or unable to cooperate, the entire effect may be lost. The reason is quite plain. At an extremely low dynamic level — a mere breath of tone — a single instrument being played piano or mezzo forte may actually equal the volume of sound produced by all of the other instruments. Some individual players will always react negatively to suggestions of this sort, taking the attitude perhaps that the conductor is "too particular"; and it is these few students who make the attainment of really fine results difficult and sometimes impossible.

The conductor should decide beforehand which parts are most important and most interesting, and these parts should be made to stand out from the harmonic, melodic, and rhythmic background. The actual technique of accomplishing this is merely that of establishing dynamic contrast by having the important material played louder or by having the less important material played softer. If the problem involves a contrast in tone color or tone quality, the solution is usually suggested by the instrumentation. Illustrations of the overbalancing of essential and interesting material by harmonic noise may be found in many of the overtures written for young bands. The following will illustrate:

The basses, trombones, baritones, bassoons, and low saxophones are massed on the melody which they attack with undisguised ferocity; but they are no match for the much larger number of clarinets, flutes, piccolos, oboes, cornets, horns, and saxophones which pound out a sort of harmonic drum part through a total range of about three octaves, all above the range of the melody instruments. The most satisfactory remedy would be to avoid this type of music, but if this is not always possible, the next best solution is to reduce the number of instruments assigned to the accompaniment part and to instruct these sections to play no louder than mezzo forte with a fairly sharp attack on the first note of each measure, all other notes to be played staccato. The melody parts should be well-sustained throughout. With careful treatment such passages may be made to sound somewhat less banal than they actually are.

In applying such corrective measures as may seem to be indicated it is essential that the conductor have a very fine appreciation of dynamic values, especially with reference to the type of part which will be easily submerged or that which may be permitted to stand out boldly without jeopardizing other parts. For example, the bassoon in all registers, the flute in its lower register, sometimes the baritone horn, and frequently the viola are heard with difficulty against almost any kind of harmonic background. In contrast, the listener seldom fails to hear the cornet, the first violin, the oboe, or the flute and the clarinet in their upper registers. These are only the most obvious illustrations. There are many exceptions, depending upon the manner in which the parts are written. If the tendency is toward the loss of a distinctive part in the tonal mass, everything possible should be done to insure the important voices being heard, and heard *easily*. The listener should never be compelled to concentrate too intently upon the solo part in order to keep it separated from other parts. The melodies should be delivered to the listener; he should not be required to come for them himself. One astute conductor suggests to his students that there is always one member of the audience who is a little hard of hearing, and who is neither very musical nor very much interested in what the performers are doing. Strangely enough this difficult customer always sits in the back row of the auditorium. It is to him that the band or the orchestra is playing. Now the point of this is not that the group must play louder than it otherwise might, but that it play with greater *clarity* and more contrast between melody and accompaniment. This is essentially a problem in the control of dynamics. The types of writing which tend to cover other parts are those of a sustained character, especially when played by instruments in the lower and middle registers. Pizzicato, spiccato, and all forms of detached writing do not cover other parts easily and may usually be played with a fair degree of force, even against important melodies.

The question of dynamic balance and contrast has been treated thus far chiefly with reference to the relationship between the various instruments and sections. This may be referred to as a "perpendicular" concept of dynamic usage. Equally important is the manner in which the law of dynamic balance and contrast are applied "horizontally"; i.e., to the melodic line. Before taking up this matter it might be well to consider a question which has proved somewhat confusing to many amateur players. This question was stated rather facetiously, but very pointedly, by a high school student when he asked, "How loud is loud?" The more this question is studied the more one begins to realize that perhaps the conductors of instrumental groups have been expecting too much of their students in the interpretation of dynamic indications. For a practical solution of this obvious difficulty two things are required – a workable definition of dynamic differences and actual practice in producing tones at the various levels.

Unless we wish to go entirely scientific and measure tone in terms of decibels, or units of sound intensity, we must accept a definition which is sufficiently flexible to apply equally to all of the instruments and one which can be understood and applied by the average student. To meet these requirements the following definition is suggested: The difference between one dynamic degree and the one adjacent to it in the common usage (*pp—p—mp* or *mf—f—ff*) is that amount of change in intensity which may be *easily recognized* by the untrained listener. This definition undoubtedly leaves many technical loopholes, but it applies quite acceptably to the problem at hand, which is to secure from the student player a specific reaction to each of the commonly used dynamic symbols. In actual practice the student will extend this range from the softest tone which it is possible for him to produce to the loudest within his capacity, and he will manage a fairly accurate distribution within these extremes. To develop a uniform response which may be utilized in the ensemble rehearsals the conductor should drill his students as individuals, in sections, and in the full ensemble in the production of these various levels. The conductor may find it convenient to refer to the levels by number, from one (pianissimo) to five (fortissimo). It is understood that mezzo piano and mezzo forte are essentially the same, with the latter in more common use. Ensemble drill in dynamic treatment, using simple chords as a basis, is both interesting and instructive; and the players soon acquire a reasonably accurate conception of the different levels of intensity.

As a part of the drill process suggested above, both the crescendo and the decrescendo should be practiced. These are difficult media of expression and involve an unusual degree of technical control. A common fault in this phase of dynamic variation is what is known as the "stair step" crescendo. Even organizations which can produce a perfectly balanced and controlled crescendo in the drill process fall into the bad habit of employing the stair step technique in performance. This fault is most noticeable when a crescendo is combined with a series of half notes or whole notes in a slow tempo. Each tone in the series is played successively louder until the peak of the crescendo is reached, but the increase is attained through a succession of "jerks" or "jumps" in dynamic intensity. This produces a distorted effect, not at all in accord with the intended character of the crescendo. When properly executed, any given tone in the series will start at the dynamic level of the preceding tone but will increase to a higher level as it is sustained, thus producing a gradual increase throughout the passage — an "escalator" crescendo instead of a "stair step" crescendo.

A great many students, and not a few conductors, seem unaware of the commonly accepted rule that a dynamic indication appearing in the part remains effective until some other marking is inserted. In many cases the rule is known but ignored, and as players and conductors become increasingly careless in this matter, the fine points of dynamic form are thrown into the discard. An extended pianissimo passage may terminate in a robust forte, an abrupt drop from fortissimo to pianissimo may be heard as a limping, characterless decrescendo, and a forte-piano (*fp*) may not even be observed. Dynamic indications are important, and they should be studied and interpreted with meticulous care. When it is obvious that the printed indications should be modified, it is the privilege, nay, the responsibility, of the conductor to make such changes; but these alterations should always be in strict conformity with the spirit of the composition and the intent of the composer insofar as that can be determined. Arrangers and editors are frequently careless in this matter, and a great many of the so-called school editions are both inadequately and incorrectly marked as regards the dynamic values.

The modifications usually required to insure a correct balance of parts may often be more a matter of common understanding between the players and the conductor than one requiring actual remarking of the dynamics. The brass instruments will usually play somewhat softer than the parts indicate, except for special effects; the flutes will play louder, as a rule; all of the smaller sections except the brasses will interpret their dynamics on the loud side; and the "second" sections (Violin II, Clarinet II-III, Cornet II, etc.) will usually make no mistake by playing with fairly full volume of tone. These are general suggestions only and they do not apply to special situations involving solo passages and intricate light ensemble playing.

A special form of dynamic modification has been employed by some conductors in the treatment of the full wind chords which frequently appear in the classical overtures and some of the symphony movements of the same period. These chords are usually sustained against a running part in the strings, but if they are played with the full force which is indicated, the string parts are sure to be covered completely. The effect which was obviously intended by the composer can be obtained by having the wind instruments attack these chords with the force indicated and immediately subside to about a mezzo forte, sustaining at this level. The employment of this device adds clarity and restraint to the performance and does not violate the dictates of good taste or tradition.

Because there are so many details of performance in which the technical and the interpretative aspects must be considered as one, any discussion of dynamic problems must necessarily touch upon elements of interpretation. For example, there is the problem of phrase endings. As one conductor says to his students on occasion, "Do not send the phrase on its way with a kick, but kiss it good-bye!" Besides illustrating the technique of a great teacher, this reference illustrates the relationship between dynamic treatment and expression. The common habit of "clipping," or "exploding" the phrase endings shows both a lack of tonal control and an unhappy concept of musical values. The conductor can attack such problems from either the mechanical or the aesthetic angle, or from both at the same time, but the essential point is that no fine interpretative results can be obtained without the presence of a sensitivity to dynamic values.

A somewhat similar detail is that of short swells (*crescendo* and *decrescendo*) within a longer phrase. The dynamic level of the phrase within which the swell occurs will determine the extent of the increase. To exaggerate in such cases would be to destroy entirely the character of the passage. In the same manner, any accent or sforzando should be held reasonably well within the dynamic range which governs the particular passage. Should something more than an accent be desired by the composer within a passage marked piano or pianissimo, he will indicate forte-piano or even fortissimo-pianissimo for emphasis. The *forte-piano* is one of the truly delightful effects when it is executed cleanly, with proper elasticity and with a perfectly controlled sustained piano following the forte.

Still another problem in dynamic balance is that involved in the repetition of a melodic figure by several different sections of individual players. This requires not only the imitation of phrasing, articulation, bowing, or rhythm, but also a proper relationship in the matter of dynamic force. The following excerpt illustrates the use of exact duplication of rhythm and melody with a slight modification of tonal volume:

SYMPHONY No. V IN E MINOR – SCHERZO – DVORAK (Orchestra)

(Partial score only.)

It would be quite impossible to include in this text examples of all of the different types of dynamic problems. Such an undertaking would fill many large volumes, and it is doubtful whether anything like a comprehensive selection could be made. The best source-books for this type of material must always remain the scores themselves, in which every conceivable variety of dynamic treatment may be found. A few excerpts are included here, however, for the purpose of illustrating some of the more common problems which may be encountered by the school band or orchestra conductor.

The following example shows the crescendo in one voice against diverse moving parts in other voices. To be played effectively, this crescendo must be carried to a full forte and the drop to piano must be very abrupt. All other parts should be held to a restrained piano. Incidentally, this passage illustrates a problem in timing and technical control which most amateurs find extremely difficult — the tied quarter and sixteenth note, followed by tongued sixteenth notes. Rigidly exact counting and very precise articulation are the points to be stressed in playing this figure. The passage would be even more difficult for string players.

CHORAL PRELUDE "WE ALL BELIEVE IN ONE GOD" – BACH (Band)

Copyright by Music Publishers Holding Corp., New York
Reprinted by permission

(These parts are doubled by other woodwind instruments.)

The abbreviated contrapuntal effect in the following excerpt is very effective, provided the first two measures of each voice enter with full tone and a strong accent. Many amateurs, and some professionals, make a practice of shortening all accented notes. While this device might be employed effectively in certain types of street marches, it should not be used carelessly or indiscriminately. In this instance, the notes should be sustained for their full values.

"ARIANE" OVERTURE – BOYER (Band)

The following excerpt illustrates the complexities involved in coordinating several independent voices, each carrying a more or less independent rhythm. The entrance of each new voice must be marked by a very slight attack and the articulation must be clarified by the use of the same device. This should not be overdone, however.

"CHANT FROM THE GREAT PLAINS" – BUSCH (Band)

Passages of this type demand absolute independence on the part of the individual players, since no rhythmic or melodic support is provided by other sections and there is nothing in the way of harmonic background to cover any mistakes that might be made. Each player is strictly "on his own". The common lack of rhythmic independence may explain the limited use of more involved musical material of this type, or this lack may be the direct result of too much dependence upon thickly-arranged and rhythmically elementary marches, overtures, and short pieces.

This example shows how carefully the great Russian symphonist indicated the dynamic treatment of melodic line and accompanying parts:

SYMPHONY No.V IN E MINOR – ANDANTE CANTABILE – Tschaikówsky
(Orchestra)

(Other parts are marked in a like manner.)

By permission of Associated Music Publishers, Inc., New York.

Constant vigilance must characterize the conductor's approach to the twin problems of balance and dynamic contrast, for these are the elements that determine which of the musical material will be heard. Closely related, and of equal importance, is the problem of intonation. Balance, contrast, and intonation — these are the elements which give clarity, force, and intelligibility to the performance. A high degree of individual playing skill avails nothing unless the individuals can play together — in tune and in balance. However profound or brilliant may be the conductor's concept of interpretation, the musical product will be unsatisfactory unless the players have the capacity to translate these ideas into tone. Problems of individual technic, reading, ensemble tone quality, intonation, and balance should be relegated to the realm of the habitual as early as possible in order that the rehearsals may be given over largely to the much more interesting work of interpretation, and the enjoyment of the best musical literature.

Probably the last word in regard to dynamic indications has been spoken by Bizet in his *L'Arlesienne Suite, No 1*. The following excerpt is interesting principally for the great dynamic contrast for which it calls, but many scores which contain fewer markings make infinitely more subtle demands upon the players and, incidentally, upon the conductor.

L'ARLESIENNE SUITE NO. 1. PRELUDE   BIZET.

E.E. 3842

By permission of Associated Music Publishers, Inc., New York.

CHAPTER XV

Interpretation

To be a successful teacher of amateurs one must believe thoroughly that everything related to musical performance *can be taught*. The teacher who enters upon his task with certain mental reservations will be successful only in proportion to the extent of the qualifications which exist in his own mind. If he is convinced that technical progress can be made only up to a given point, if he assumes that false intonation is a condition of amateur performance, or if he feels that he must confine his choice of material to easy "pieces," his eventual success will be governed by these considerations. Unlimited faith in the latent technical and musical capacity of his students must always be the solid foundation upon which a successful teaching career in the field of instrumental music is predicated. In answer to any who might raise a protest to this assertion one has only to point to the many teachers and conductors of school organizations who have produced almost professional results with ordinary student material under ordinary conditions of training. These teachers have had faith in the ability of their students to learn, and perhaps more important in the final analysis, they have had faith in their own ability to teach.

Most teachers are willing to accept, in theory at least, the fact that basic playing techniques can be taught to most normal children. This naturally rules out the possibility of doing much for those who are tone deaf, those who suffer a like deficiency in rhythmic impulse, those who are physically or muscularly unsuited to a particular instrument, and those whose general intelligence is so low that they would fail in any other activity. The attainment of an acceptable level of technical ability must also be conditioned by the amount of time available for instruction and practice and the availability of satisfactory equipment and material. Many teachers who admit the possibility of their students' acquiring a high degree of technical skill decline to accept the principle that interpretation can be taught.

189

Possibly one reason for this is that these teachers have devoted so large a proportion of their time to the mastery of playing techniques that they have neglected to study the problems related to the teaching of interpretation. It may even be true that an erroneous conception of teaching *sequence* is the source of the difficulty — the reasoning that physical skills should be taught first, then the interpretative skills. This division of emphasis is fatal to any balanced progress in music education. All of the essential skills must be taught concurrently in order that one may support the others and give purpose and direction to the entire process.

In searching out the reasons for the failure of so many teachers to teach interpretation one is almost forced to the conclusion that this failure is traceable to the fact that the interpretative values are hidden values, whereas the purely technical problems appear on the surface. The quotation attributed to Robert Schumann, "Tone is the gold for which the true artist mines deepest," applies with equal force to the elements of expression and interpretation. If the teacher himself is not extremely sensitive to the interpretative qualities of the compositions to be performed, or if he does not devote sufficient study to this phase of his task, it is not surprising that the players themselves should regard interpretation as of secondary importance. The teacher must "mine deeply" for the emotional, spiritual, descriptive, or dramatic elements which may be hidden far under the surface of mere note sequences and rhythmic patterns; and he must come up with enough shining nuggets to arouse the interest and enthusiasm of his students. They must be convinced that there are still more hidden treasures which they themselves can find if they, in turn, are willing to mine deeply. Interpretation is not the exclusive property of the conductor; it must be shared with every student in the group, and the students must be encouraged to believe that they are prospectors for, as well as miners of, this musical wealth. The conductor will have advanced far toward his goal of building a complete pedagogical structure when he accepts the theory that expression can be taught. His next important step will be to develop the actual techniques required in the teaching of this extremely elusive element in musical performance.

If one were called upon to prepare an original textbook on the playing of the violin, for example, he would analyze carefully all of the available literature for the instrument, and he would study with more real purpose than ever before the actual movements which were required in the playing of the violin. In this process of research he would be seeking fundamental principles. He would endeavor to isolate the essential elements in the technique of the instrument, and he would ignore such items as were merely decorative or incidental. Having assembled all of his facts, he would then proceed to organize these facts into logical categories and in proper sequence; and finally, the actual writing of the text would be undertaken.

A relatively small number of musicians have written methods for the violin or for other instruments, but a very large proportion of those engaged in the teaching of instrumental music have, at one time or another, devoted themselves to some form of research or investigation very similar to that which would be required for the writing of such a text. How few of these practical musicians and scholars within the field of music have ever devoted an equivalent amount of study to the organization and the mastery of the technique of interpretation!* Interpretation and expression are elements which are taken too much for granted throughout the profession. Occasionally a conductor will check the tempi of a composition against a commercial recording, or he may compare his interpretation with that of some other orchestra or band, but seldom does he make a detailed study of the hidden elements of expression and devise teaching techniques which will insure a correct response on the part of his players. One suspects that the average conductor of a school orchestra or band does not regard study of this kind as essential; or perhaps the explanation is that he does not have sufficient time for working out both the technical and the interpretative elements in performance. A few conductors undoubtedly have such an excellent background of preparation that special study of interpretation is not necessary, but it would seem that even these might find such analysis helpful in clarifying the presentation of these problems.

Interpretation has been defined by a high school student as "what the players do to the music to make it interesting." This definition would hardly merit inclusion in the standard dictionary, but it does express the commonly accepted idea regarding the subject. Something must be done to the music to give it vitality and color, and

---

* An exhaustive treatment of interpretative elements, with copious illustrations from standard orchestral literature, is contained in "Handbook of Conducting" by Hermann Scherchen (Oxford University Press).

it is the task of the conductor to discover what this something is and how best to induce the players in the organization to react in such manner as to bring about the desired result.

The system of notation which is now employed may have some shortcomings, but it is by far the best system ever invented, and in general, it serves its purpose well. Yet how inadequate is this or any other system when the rigidity of the printed symbols is compared with the flexibility of the actual performance! The printed part becomes merely a point of departure where the finer points of expression are concerned. The term ritardando, for example, tells nothing about either the rate or the extent of change in tempo. This choice must be left to the judgment and discretion of the performer or the conductor. Even the quarter notes within a single measure are subject to artistic variation. The tonal coloring of a chord may be controlled by emphasis upon certain voices. A given passage may be made either ponderous or light by different treatments, but in both cases the printed notes are the same. The reader will call to mind any number of instances in which the actual performance is at variance with the printed score, but if there still remains any question concerning the matter, a few simple experiments with a standard recording, a conductor's score, and a metronome will provide the answer. Interpretation is, in its essence, *controlled deviation* from the printed score.

It is just at this point that some confusion is apt to arise. The artist-conductor modifies the tempo and the dynamics or readjusts the phrasing to suit his taste, and no objections are raised; the musical product is a pleasure and a delight. The inartistic imitator applies the same technique with results which are quite disastrous. Interpretation, in his clumsy hands, becomes mutilation. The difference between the two is much more complex than appears on the surface, and it involves background, native intelligence, emotional stability, musical understanding, conducting skill, judgment, discrimination, restraint, and a great many other elements of education and character which are delicately interwoven into the personality of the individuals. It is important that each conductor should know his own capacities and his own limitations and that he be guided by this knowledge. If, in a given instance, the conductor recognizes a tendency to *over*-interpret, it would be best for him to adhere rather strictly to the score, following the prescribed tempi, tempo modifications, dynamics, and phrasings. If, on the other hand, he realizes that his approach is inclined to be stolid and academic, he might make a conscious effort to attain a somewhat more flexible and carefree reading. Such decisions must always be made with strict reference to the type of composition to be presented and the natural tendencies of the organization which is performing the work. Occasionally the conductor may find it necessary to supply an element of restraint which is lacking in the players, or he might find it advisable to inject even a slight overdose of vitality into a performance which is threatened with stagnation and ultimate artistic death.

One of the conductor's first objectives should be to make the performance of the music as interesting as possible to the players, and to accomplish this purpose he should make use of musical material which has a strong natural appeal. Much dull music has been written and published, and much that appears to be dull can be made exciting and inspiring in the hands of a conductor who knows how to accomplish this end. The best guide is always the music itself. If the conductor understands thoroughly the form of the composition, the historical, social, or dramatic situation which gave rise to its creation, and the exact manner in which it must be performed for maximum effectiveness, the players are almost sure to respond with enthusiasm. Too often the students are asked to *play notes* when their natural desire is to *make music*. It is the conductor's task to "set the stage" for every number that is played, and if this is done with proper enthusiasm and interest on his part, the players will actually recreate the spirit which impelled the composer. This is one means, and probably the best, of insuring adequacy in interpretation. One of the characteristics of amateur performance is that it is vital and whole-hearted. The professional may play the notes with greater accuracy, but the amateur will invest the work with spontaneity, freshness, and verve. It is this quality in amateur performance which constitutes the chief reward of the conductor, but it can be brought to the surface only by a conductor who selects his program material with care and who possesses the ability to stimulate the correct response on the part of the players.

Music is as broad in its scope as humanity itself. Every human emotion finds its expression in music, and through the performance of music these emotions can be recreated in the listener. Thus we see the completion of a cycle — a mood or an emotion captured by the composer, reproduced by the performer, and reflected in the emotional response of the listener. Unless the conductor interprets the score with fidelity and understanding this cycle is broken and the listener receives an impression entirely different from that originally registered upon the composer and transmitted by him to posterity. The existence of this cycle suggests that the source to which the conductor must go for his inspiration and his information is always the point of origin. To fully appreciate the works of Haydn, for example, one must know something about his life, his personality, the little court in which he was employed, and the nature of the orchestra for which his works were written. The works of Bach and the manner of playing them might have become grossly distorted had there not been, down through the years, honest and sincere musicians who had dedicated their lives to the preservation of these works in their original form. The Strauss waltzes lean heavily upon tradition and the social atmosphere which prevailed at the time they were written. These examples will suggest a long list of works, the correct performance of which demands of the conductor a somewhat detailed knowledge of music history, particularly as it touches upon the form in which these works are written, and the social, historical, and family backgrounds of their composers. The acquisition of this body of information must be the first step in the process of perfecting a technique of interpretation.

To list but a few of the various types of music will suggest the immense scope of the materials with which the conductor might reasonably be expected to be familiar. In addition to the standard symphonic literature there are the classical suites and overtures, the opera, incidental music of the theater including the ballet, folksongs and folk-dances, sacred music, music for solo instruments with orchestra, descriptive music including such works as Tschaikowsky's *1812 Overture*, national and patriotic music including works of the type of the Sibelius *Finlandia*, absolute and abstract music, children's songs and dances, martial music including quickstep marches, ceremonial marches, atmospheric music with or without a program, and the music of the modern dance which could only by a great stretch of the imagination be classified as folk-music. With such a wealth of musical material available, the conductors of school orchestras and bands should experience little difficulty in selecting music of real significance. The problem of interpretation will be made infinitely easier if the music which is used possesses a distinctive character and if it has back of it a rich tradition.

The conductor's choice of musical material will be governed to some extent by the capacity of his organization. If the group is in the process of making the acquaintance of the masterworks, the emphasis should be upon those which are strongly rhythmic and melodic; the more sedate andante movements of the symphonies may be reserved until such time as the orchestra is ready to accept them with enthusiasm. Unfortunately, there is little material available for band comparable to the symphonic andante. The band director will experience somewhat less difficulty in holding the interest of a young group due to the fact that the chief problems in the band literature are technical rather than musical in nature.

Having selected music which lends itself well to varied and interesting forms of interpretation, and having studied this material carefully in the light of its interpretative value, the conductor faces the problem of transmitting his ideas effectively to the members of his group. It is one thing to discuss mechanical processes before an organization and to secure from the players a specific response on matters involving technic, counting, or tonal balance, but quite a different thing to elicit from these same players just the right turn of a phrase or the exact inflection or nuance which may be required to produce the desired *expressive* quality. It is precisely this point at which many conductors fail completely, and unless these unfortunate individuals are able to discover some method of communicating their ideas of interpretation to their players, their success as conductors will be negligible. No substitute has as yet been found for fine expression. Mechanical skill, however great, cannot breathe life and spirit into a performance. Virtuosity is not music, and the average listener would rather hear a simple melody, played with warmth and feeling, than a "display piece" replete with finger gymnastics and brass pyrotechnics.

The conductor may have a perfectly clear conception of how a given melody should be played and his emotional reaction may be precisely the correct one, but his problem is to convey this mental and emotional picture to the performer by the simplest and most direct method. The congenital instrumentalist will no doubt be greatly disappointed by the suggestion which is offered for the solution of this problem; namely, that the conductor *sing* the melody in question. The objections which will be raised to this method are that most instrumentalists cannot sing, that a melody badly sung had better not be sung at all, that the conductor should not be expected to suffer the embarrassment of singing alone before his group, that many instrumental idioms cannot be sung, that the range of the human voice is too limited, *et cetera, ad infinitum.* To all of these objections there is only one answer, namely, that most of the successful conductors do sing on occasion, however badly, and that this seems to be the only direct method. One well-known conductor meets the problem by whistling, but he whistles very badly. Others try to play the melodies on an instrument, but this is not always satisfactory and it wastes valuable time.

Whether the dyed-in-the-wool instrumentalist cares to admit it or not, the fact remains that song is the real basis of all music. The player of a brass instrument "sings" through his horn, and if the result is not song-like in character, he has failed to this extent. The only exceptions to this are the relatively few brass passages which are essentially percussive in character — fanfares, staccato passages, and solid chordal structures. The woodwinds, as well as the strings, employ a modified vocal idiom in a very large proportion of their playing. It is extremely likely that the general failure of instrumental organizations to attain the same degree of excellence in the field of interpretation that these groups have attained in technical skill may be traced to the neglect of their conductors to emphasize the importance of song as a basis of interpretation.

No method of instruction has ever entirely supplanted that of trial and error. Mistakes in technic and interpretation cannot always be avoided; in fact, they sometimes serve an extremely useful purpose in illustrating to the student what not to do. One of the most successful instrumental directors frequently calls upon his group to deliberately play a given passage in the wrong manner. By the use of this device he gives the students a vivid and unforgettable picture of the error of their ways. Furthermore, the students enjoy the humor of this approach, and there is never any question as to the efficacy of the cure. The trial-and-error method is an effective means of helping the student to decide which of several choices of interpretation is best. Thus he is developing his own taste and his own judgment. He probably concentrates somewhat more intently upon the problem at hand when he knows that he must be the one to decide the issue, and through this process he acquires a quicker grasp of new interpretative problems.

A very large proportion of the difficulties which appear on the surface as problems of expression or interpretation may actually be corrected by means of a slightly different technical treatment. Deficiencies in accenting fall within this classification, as do special problems related to the use of the staccato, phrasing, and articulation. It is unimportant whether any given problem be regarded as a technical or as an interpretative problem so long as the proper remedy be found for the difficulty. Most of the complications in the field of expression do, in fact, require a solution which is based upon either the mechanics of playing or upon a combination of tempo or accent with a particular technique.

The use of exaggeration is one of the most practical devices in the teaching of musical expression. Just as the teacher of dramatic art gains the desired response by requiring the student to caricature, or *over*-act, a given part, the orchestra or band conductor will often secure the precise musical effect he wishes by asking a player, or a section, to exaggerate the effect which he suggests. For example, a real pianissimo may sometimes be obtained, when all other methods have failed, by the absurd request that the strings merely *pretend* to play. The students are quick to catch the implication of this suggestion and they will usually produce the pianissimo about as desired. A similar device has been used effectively in teaching the violins to play the spiccato bowing. The conductor has the players set their bows upon the string at the precise spot at which he knows a bounce is most likely to result, and he then instructs the players to move the bows rapidly back and forth but not under any circumstance to permit the bow to bounce! After a few strokes the spiccato is heard in spite of the students' best efforts to prevent it. What actually happens is that the very restraint which the teacher suggested is an essential part of the spiccato technique. This method of teaching by suggestion, by opposites, and by contrasts is perfectly legitimate, and its application to the presentation of interpretative problems is practically limitless.

To obtain the best results and incidentally to obtain the most real pleasure and enjoyment from the rehearsal the conductor should select music which is colorful and distinctive — music which tells a story, suggests a mood, depicts a dramatic situation, or arouses a strong emotional reaction. With proper preliminary discussion of the music's character or setting the players will enter wholeheartedly into the spirit of such a work and will interpret it with unbelievable fervor. Young players cannot resist this type of approach. This is self-expression at its best, and all of the drudgery of mechanics and technic is forgotten in the pleasure of having something to say and being able to say it in the glorious manner.

It must be recognized that many orchestras and bands do not react to the performance of music in this way. In contests, and sometimes in concerts, one observes the stolid expression and the tense posture so characteristic of a certain type of leadership. One may be reasonably sure that any organization which has this do-or-die attitude toward the task at hand is not getting a great deal of permanent value from its rehearsals. Music must be enjoyed before much profit can be derived from its practice. No concert or other public appearance is worth the cost unless the player can go onto the platform with a smiling face and a normal pulse. If the student's attitude toward the activity is correct, and if the conductor's attitude toward his students is correct, there should be no need for the mental, physical, and emotional stress which is so often observed in the work of amateur groups. The relationship between attitude and interpretation is much closer than is ordinarily appreciated because both have their source in the personality of the conductor. If his attitude is the reflection of a sound educational philosophy, his interpretations will be fundamentally right, for the interpretation of life and the interpretation of music spring from the common source of human sympathy and understanding.

As has been stated earlier in this chapter, the principal elements in performance upon which expression or interpretation depend are those which are variable in character. One of the most important of these factors is that of tempo. In some compositions exact metronomic indications are given, but in many others this matter is left largely to the discretion of the conductor. The practical value of the metronomic markings is limited by the fact that these indications occasionally represent the opinion of an editor who may be much less of a musician than the conductor who will prepare and present the work. Even where such indications have been inserted by the composer there is ample justification for questioning their accuracy, or at least their musical effectiveness. Strange as it may seem, composers have not always been the best interpreters of their own works, and furthermore, the choice of a tempo may depend to some extent upon the manner in which a composition is performed. For example, an allegro which is played with an extremely elastic beat and in a crisp, vital style might actually give the impression of being played faster than the same movement played at the same tempo but in a more legato manner. The actual metronomic tempo may, therefore, be said to depend somewhat upon the style in which the composition is played, and as previously pointed out, there is no exact means of indicating the playing style with the system of notation now in use.

Wagner, in his book "On Conducting," states that the correct tempo of any given melody will be dictated by the nature of the melody itself. It was his firm conviction that any well-written melody could be played properly at only one tempo. In his own words, "The right comprehension of the melody is the sole guide to the right tempo; these two things are inseparable: the one implies and qualifies the other." Wagner further suggests that the conductor's "choice of tempo will show whether he understands the piece or not" and that "correct tempo induces correct phrasing and expression."

Certainly it may be said that, in their choice of tempi, a great many conductors have met their musical and interpretative Waterloos. Extreme care must always be exercised in this matter and also with reference to any *changes* in tempo that might be suggested by the melody within a given passage. If, for example, one portion of an extended allegro is to be played at a somewhat slower tempo in order to permit of a more legato treatment of melodic material, this change should be very slight and it should be held well within the limits of the term *allegro*. In other words, a basic tempo may be bent but never broken.

Another variable element is that embodied in tempo changes suggested by such terms as ritardando, rallentando, accelerando, meno mosso, and piu mosso. Here again there is no way of knowing precisely how much slower or how much faster the movement should be taken. The degree of change must always rest with the conductor. A careful study of the nature of the melody and the mood of the composition will prove helpful, as will a knowledge of the tradition of the particular work. To know the tradition one must have heard the composition played under the direction of recognized conductors.

Still another form of tempo change is the rubato. This term (which means, literally, "robbed") is seldom printed in the score, but it is used to describe those slight modifications of tempo which the conductor indicates by his beat, sometimes within the limits of a single measure. The assumption is that any hurrying of the movement at one point is balanced by a slackening of tempo elsewhere. This expressive device must be handled with extreme care in order not to destroy the basic flow of the tempo. When the rubato is exaggerated, or when it is applied inappropriately, the conductor earns the sobriquet, "a tempo rubato conductor." The device must always be used with the utmost moderation and discretion.

The fermata (⌢) and the tenuto (ten.) are tempo change indications which apply to single notes, or in the case of the fermata, to rests. The former usually implies a marked pause, or hold, at the point indicated and the latter merely a slight delay on a given note. Both are variable, their duration depending upon the artistic judgment of the conductor. The "break" (♩ ♩ // ♩) is just what the term implies, a very slight pause between two notes, the time required for the pause not being taken from the full time of the measure but representing only a slight cessation of movement.

A good deal of confusion exists with reference to those indications which affect the duration of single notes or the manner in which they are to be played. Following are some of the more common forms:

The attempts which have been made to clarify the meanings of these various markings have been none too successful, largely because the indications have different interpretations for different instruments and because of the difficulty of making such fine distinctions in note duration.

Following are the more commonly accepted interpretations of the above markings:

(A) Notes which bear no mark of any kind should be bowed or tongued separately and they should presumably receive full value.

(B) All notes embraced by the slur should be included on one bow or within one "tongue group"; i.e., the tongue articulates the first note only, there being no further action of the tongue until the start of a new slurred group or a separate note.

(C) The value of these notes is reduced by approximately one half and a separate bow or tongue attack is used for each. In string music the dot is used to indicate the staccato and the spiccato bowing styles.

(D) This form may mean one thing for a stringed instrument and quite a different thing for a wind instrument. For the former it still implies either a staccato or a spiccato, but the sequence must be played with the bow moving in the same direction. For the wind instrument this form suggests that the notes are less sharply detached than in Form C.

(E) These notes are to be played with separate bows or tongue strokes but with a broadening emphasis and a very slight separation between notes. In practice notes so marked usually receive a definite pulsation of such length as the beat permits.

(F) This form is the same as the preceding one, except that all notes are played on one bow or tongue.

(G) The acute mark implies that these notes are to be played as short as possible and with considerable force, although the basic dynamic indication will control the volume to some extent.

(H) This form is the one which is surrounded with the most mystery. What it seems to indicate is: Play the notes long, with a slight separation and an impulse, but also short — about half the value indicated!

In general the interpreter will not have too much difficulty in following these markings, but if the player of a wind instrument should come upon such a composite sequence as the following:

one wonders just what the actual performance would be like. Could the listener distinguish between the various forms?

In a preceding chapter (pp. 116-117) the common failure of players to sustain notes to their full value was mentioned briefly, but for the sake of completeness in the treatment of the subject under consideration this question merits further attention. The problem is best illustrated by reference to the almost universal failure to give the dotted half note in a slow four beat measure its full value. This rhythmic figure (♩. ♩) requires that the tone be sustained *throughout* three complete beats, stopping at the *end* of the third beat or the exact beginning of the fourth. In such cases the beat must be thought of as having duration.

A somewhat similar weakness is observed in the manner in which many groups treat the whole note in choral-like numbers characterized by a succession of sustained chords. Due to carelessness in the matter of breath control and the well-established habit of "clipping" the phrase endings, such compositions usually lose much of the sustained character which they should possess. One conductor instructs his wind players to take breath at any other point *except* at the close of those phrases which should carry over to the next without perceptible break.

The same sort of smooth transition should be employed frequently in melodic passages in which fragments of melody are assigned alternately to various sections or individual players. Students, and professional players as well, are inclined to shorten the close of such melodic bits, thus leaving a gap in the tone before the entrance of the new voice. This common practice suggests a lack of appreciation of the importance of good ensemble, or teamwork. The solution is quite simple if the proper teaching technique is applied. The best device yet discovered is to ask one member of the group to hand a pencil, or any other object, to another member of the group. In this transfer it is observed that at one point both students have their hands on the object. Exactly the same thing should occur in passing a melody from one player to another. The weakness of the other method may be effectively demonstrated by throwing, or tossing, the object from one student to another. This may strike some conductors as a childish and silly teaching device, but the only important consideration is whether or not it serves its purpose.

Technic, as such, has been so strongly emphasized that in the performance of school instrumental organizations the mechanics of playing frequently stand out above the musical elements. One of the best illustrations of this is to be found in the manner in which students usually treat the triplet figure, especially where it occurs in a slow tempo. They seem to regard the triplet as a rhythmic pattern having no relationship to other parts of the melody or other rhythmic patterns with which it may be used. In the great majority of instances the triplet is played too quickly and with too sharp an accent on the first note. This destroys completely the broad, singing character of the figure which is almost always intended when it is used in slow time. The following example is one of many which might be chosen to illustrate this point in expression, or rather in accuracy of reading:

"ARIANE" OVERTURE – BOYER (Band)

The conductor will usually find it helpful to ask the players to deliberately *broaden* the triplet figure, giving a slight pulsation to each of the three notes. In fact, it would be far more effective to play the triplet and the duplet following as an equal five note figure than to play the separate groups in the usual manner — a "dancing" triplet followed by a legato duplet.

Another fairly common fault in the treatment of note values arises in connection with the use of the accent (>). This symbol directs the player to attack the note with special force, but it says nothing whatever about *shortening* the note. In practice, any accented note is usually given less than its full value unless, of course, the accented note is connected with another note by a slur or a tie. This careless habit may result from the fact that the accent is frequently employed in passages which suggest a detached style of playing, but the conductor should check its use carefully and make certain that no unauthorized reduction in note values results from the use of the accent.

As has been pointed out earlier in this chapter, the interpretation of the printed score rests largely upon those elements in performance which are variable in character. One is not permitted to change the key relationships of a composition, or to alter the pitch or the basic rhythmic arrangement of the notes. The instrumentation of standard works should not be tampered with, nor should the phrasing and articulation. These constitute the fixed elements in the composition which, it must be assumed, represent the considered choices of the composer. Beyond this point, largely due to the fact that the composer possessed no adequate device for extending his domination, the conductor becomes a creative artist. He is still responsible to the composer, but he is allowed a certain latitude for the exercise of his own originality and his own artistry. His field is the field of the variables — tempo (with definite restrictions) and dynamics. As we have seen, the general question of tempo includes a wide variety of minor considerations which have a direct bearing upon interpretation. The same is true of dynamic treatment. This includes all such matters as balance, crescendo, decrescendo, and accentuation.

The term "accentuation," as employed here, refers to the use of accent as a medium of expression. This does not mean accent in a limited sense, but rather, any form of pulsation or change in dynamic force which may have a bearing upon interpretation. A dynamic impulse may be short and elastic or it may be broad and sonorous. Perhaps the best example of accentuation, and the one which most nearly parallels its usage in music, is the accentuation of the spoken word. The great actor is great largely because of his powers of accentuation, his ability to stress the right word or the right syllable in precisely the manner which will be most effective in registering upon the listener a deep and lasting impression of the message contained in the lines of the play. The great artist in the field of music makes use of the same technique when he combines the elements of accentuation and of timing in the interpretation of a musical composition.

One of the most interesting and scholarly works on the subject of interpretation is one written by M. Mathis Lussy, called "Musical Expression." In this text the author treats the general subject of accentuation under three subdivisions: metrical accentuation, roughly that of the *measure;* rhythmical accentuation, that of the *phrase;* and expressive accentuation, that of *single notes* or short groups of notes. Metrical and rhythmical accentuation, as defined by Lussy, are generally well understood by musicians, but his discussion of the use of accentuation as an expressive medium opens a new and relatively unexplored field of investigation and research. This statement is not meant to suggest that the principles of expressive accentuation have not been understood and practiced by the best orchestral and band conductors but to emphasize the fact that relatively less importance has been assigned to this subject by teachers than has been accorded the more obvious problems of technic and the more usual expressive devices. The conductor will do well to examine all problems of interpretation with reference to the two variable factors which are likely to contribute most to a satisfactory result — TEMPO and DYNAMICS.

The acquisition of a trustworthy technique of interpretation is difficult principally because of the fact that the rules change with every new composition. A complete set of interpretative devices may be perfected for a given number only to be discarded or modified radically for another. Each new composition is a law unto itself, and while it is true that the same general principles apply to all like musical forms, the emphasis varies through a range as wide as the span of man's creative genius. No two composers have thought the same thoughts or expressed them in identically the same way, and in consequence, the conductor is compelled to approach each new interpretative problem with the adventurous spirit of the pioneer who knows not what he may find at the end of his journey.

There are certain guideposts along this path of discovery, however, which should not be disregarded. These are the relatively harmless-appearing musical terms which may be found at various points throughout the score. They should be studied and re-studied in terms of their application to the particular composition under preparation. In general, they fall into two categories: terms denoting tempi and terms denoting moods or styles. A good musical dictionary must be considered one of the essential items of equipment for the conductor. Other essential tools of the trade are scores, a baton, and — a *metronome.* Provided with these few simple items and an adequate store of factual knowledge and artistic inspiration, the conductor can face with confidence and enthusiasm his task of making young America musical.

Selected References

MUSIC THEORY AND GENERAL REFERENCE

Treatise on Harmony – J. Humphrey Anger (The Boston Music Company) 3 vol.

Study of the History of Music – Edward Dickinson (Charles Scribner's Sons)

Music Dictionary – Louis C. Elson (Oliver Ditson Company)

Modern Harmony – Foote and Spalding (The Arthur P. Schmidt Company)

Elementary Counterpoint – Percy Goetschius (G. Schirmer, Inc.)

Band's Music – Richard Franko Goldman (Pitman Publishing Corporation)

Musical Expression – M. Mathis Lussy (Novello and Company)

Discovering Music – McKinney and Anderson (American Book Company)

History of Musical Instruments – Curt Sachs (W. W. Norton, Inc.)

Practical Counterpoint – Stewart MacPherson (Joseph Williams, Ltd., London)

Art of Interweaving Melodies – Preston Ware Orem (Theodore Presser Company)

Principles of Musical Theory – Renée Longy-Miquelle (E. C. Schirmer Music Company)

New Encyclopedia of Music and Musicians – Waldo Selden Pratt (The Macmillan Company)

Music – A Science and an Art – John Redfield (Alfred A. Knopf)

CONDUCTING

Orchestral Conductor – Hector Berlioz (Carl Fischer, Inc.)

School Music Conductor – Bodengraven and Wilson (Hall and McCreary Company)

Choral Conducting – A. T. Davison (The Harvard University Press)

Eloquent Baton – Will Earhart (M. Witmark and Sons)

Art of the Choral Conductor – William J. Finn (C. C. Birchard and Company)

Essentials in Conducting – Karl Wilson Gehrkens (Oliver Ditson Company)

Handbook of Conducting – Herman Scherchen (Oxford University Press, London)

Language of the Baton – Adolf Schmid (G. Schirmer, Inc.)

On Conducting – Richard Wagner (William Reeves, London)

On Conducting – Felix Weingartner (Breitkopf and Hartel, Leipsig)

Conductor Raises His Baton – Father William J. Finn (Harper & Brothers)

ORCHESTRATION AND ARRANGING

Practical Orchestration — Arthur Olaf Andersen (C. C. Birchard and Company)

History of Orchestration — Adam Carse (E. P. Dutton and Company)

Orchestration — Cecil Forsyth (Macmillan and Company, Ltd., London)

Modern Band — Stanislao Gallo (C. C. Birchard and Company) 2 vol.

Orchestra — Ebenezer Prout (Augener, Ltd., London) 2 vol.

Principles of Orchestration — Nikolai Rimsky-Korsakoff (E. F. Kalmus, Inc.)

MUSIC IN SCHOOLS

History of Public School Music in the United States — Edward Bailey Birge (Oliver Ditson Company)

More Than a Pitchpipe — Ennis Davis (C. C. Birchard and Company)

Teaching and Administration of High School Music — Gehrkens and Dykema (C. C. Birchard and Company)

School Band and Orchestra Administration — Mark H. Hindsley (Boosey, Hawks, Belwin, Inc.)

Getting Results With School Bands — Prescott and Chidester (Paul A. Schmitt Music Company and Carl Fischer, Inc.)

Instrumental Director's Handbook — Sylvan D. Ward (Rubank, Inc.)

Music In the High School — H. R. Wilson (Silver Burdett Company)

CARE AND REPAIR OF INSTRUMENTS

Band Instrument Repairing Manual — Erick D. Brand, (Elkhart, Indiana)

Oboe Reed Making and Problems of the Oboe Player — Myron E. Russell (Holst Printing Company, Cedar Falls, Iowa)

Much helpful material will also be found in both current and back issues of music periodicals, especially those devoted primarily to the needs of teachers.

Index

A

Accentuation, 33–34, 203, 204–205
Accompaniment tone quality, 156
  (*See* Melody and accompaniment)
Achievement, a measure of interest, 54–55
Adaptability in teachers, 2–4, 11
Adjustment and care of instruments, 92–95, 102–105, 120, 128
Alternate fingerings and slide positions, 28–30
Alternating passages, 136–138
Amalgamation of strong and weak players, 41, 59
American Bandmasters Association, 87
Analysis of scores, 17, 23, 24, 140
Aptitudes of teachers, 6–8, 140
Attack, 32–33, 107–108, 118–119
Attendance, checking of, 49
Attitude between teacher and students, 9–10, 14, 16, 40–41, 55–56, 61–63, 92
Attitude toward music groups, 59–61

B

Bach *Choral Prelude*, 183
Balance
  (*See* Dynamic balance)
Balance and contrast of brass tone, 115–116
Balance and intonation, 36–37, 161–163, 187
Balanced growth in students, 14–15
Band music, 75–79
  (*See* Selection of music)
Bizet *L'Arlesienne Suite*, 188
Blend, its components, 161–162
  (*See* Ensemble tone)
Bolzoni *Menuetto*, 137–138
Bowings and fingerings, marking of, 85–86
Bowing, principles of, 95–97, 201
Boyer *Ariane* Overture, 184
Brass instruments, adjustment and care of, 120
Breath technique, 105–107, 116–117
Building interest in instrumental music, 57–59
Busch *Chant from The Great Plains*, 185

C

Cello, left-hand technique, 99
Chord tuning
  (*See* Ensemble tuning)
Clarinet mouthpiece and reed, 104

Clinics, conferences, etc., 4–5, 69–70
Comparison of wind instruments and voice, 42–43, 105–107, 114, 196
Comparison of wind and stringed instruments, 105–106
Condition of instruments
  (*See* Adjustment and care of instruments)
Conduct in rehearsal room, 50–51
  (*See* Discipline in rehearsals)
Conducting technique, 20–21
Conductor as a teacher, 8–9, 14–15, 17–18
Conductors, type of, 14–16, 19–20
Conflicting rhythmic patterns, 138–143
Contests, 62–65
Contrast and balance of brass tone, 115–116
Contrast, basis of performance, 161–162, 170–173, 176–178
Controlled deviation in interpretation, 191–193, 204
Coordination, technique of, 42, 132–133, 147
Cornet vs. Trumpet, 115–116
Correlation in teaching, 14–15
Counting, ensemble drill in, 42
Crescendo and decrescendo, 179–181

D

Deficiencies in ensemble performance, 134–144, 148, 161–162
Demands on students' time, 47
Demands on teacher's time, 4, 8–9, 17–18, 80
Detail, over-emphasis on, 42
Diagnosis of difficulties, 134
Diaphragmatic breathing
  (*See* Breath technique)
Difficult harmonizations, tuning of, 37–38
Discipline in rehearsals, 50–51, 61–62
Doubling of parts, 83
Drill, importance of, 16–17, 23–24, 39–41, 133–134, 142–143
Duration and expression marks, single notes, 200–201
Dvorak, *Symphony in E Minor*, 25–28, 174, 182
Dynamic balance, 81–83, 126–127, 154–155, 161–162, 170–180, 187
Dynamic exaggeration, 173, 187–188, 197
Dynamic imitation, 181–182
Dynamic indications, 82–83, 179, 180